MK.
14/9/2010
at Alnwick

C000303024

IN THE BEGINNING

IN THE BEGINNING

Harry Beckhough

The Book Guild Ltd
Sussex, England

First published in Great Britain in 2002 by
The Book Guild Ltd
25 High Street
Lewes, East Sussex
BN7 2LU

Copyright © Harry Beckhough 2002

The right of Harry Beckhough to be identified as the author of
this work has been asserted by him in accordance with the
Copyright, Designs and Patents Act 1988.

All rights reserved. No part of this publication may be repro-
duced, transmitted, or stored in a retrieval system, in any form or
by any means, without permission in writing from the publisher,
nor be otherwise circulated in any form of binding or cover other
than that in which it is published and without a similar condition
being imposed on the subsequent purchaser.

Typesetting in Times by
Acorn Bookwork, Salisbury, Wiltshire

Printed in Great Britain by
Bookcraft (Bath) Ltd, Avon

A catalogue record for this book is available from
The British Library.

ISBN 1 85776 618 0

CONTENTS

INTRODUCTION

The Old Testament is the most complete and comprehensive, exciting and dramatic exposé of human life in all its varied aspects. From a beginning enveloped in antique mythology, there develops religion from the primitive worship of gods of nature, to the foundation of monotheism with all its consequences. Yet underlying all is a basic ironic humour, stemming from the original, unique author of the Pentateuch, yclept J. Only one important element is missing: the possible existence of a Supreme Spirit overall, the meaning of Life itself and the revealing of our true destiny.

These are the first steps towards the unlocking of the hidden secrets of the Bible. Albeit a serious endeavour, it is nonetheless spiced from the very outset with mystery, fable, high drama, comic relief, romance, love and hate, religious movements, sinful orgies, epic battles, victories and defeats, adultery, rape, divorce, plagues, joy and grief, hope and despair, birth and death, crime and punishment. It covers the whole gamut of human life and emotions in a never-ending continuous, dynamic movement.

These first five Books of Genesis to Deuteronomy cover all life's experiences, and raise the age-old questions of whence came we, where are we now and whither are we going. Never was any book by human author so redolent of every facet of human life. The original, anonymous author J steps out of that unknown, mysterious ancient world of our primitive ancestors to give us a unique picture of his version of how it all began.

This book seeks to shed new light on the fascinating story emerging from those first chapters of our Bible, illuminating the reason why it remains the best-selling book of all time. No wonder many of our greatest authors, including Shakespeare, historians and philosophers, even writers of romantic novels and mystery thrillers, have had recourse to the Bible for some of their best material, inspirations, character studies and human portrayals.

We invite you to sharpen your appetite on this meal of many courses spread before you from the Beginning . . . .

1

IN THE BEGINNING

Can there be anything more provocative than the opening
words of the Bible? What beginning, how, when and where? Is
it fact or fiction, and who or what came first? Nothing has
produced more disputes in scientific, archaeological, philosophical, academic and religious circles than the true meaning
and concept of Genesis. Some say 'creation,' but I prefer
'birth' because that is its main concern – the birth of a great
nation. Even scientists differ in their theories of the origin of
our planet, dealing with cool detachment in billions of years.
The author was solely concerned with interpreting his own
viable solution to the eternal question of how it all began. But
there are obvious errors. A divinity who needs to rest after six
days' labour is assuredly a human imaginative concept. As
must be the unbalanced stages of succession – first our planet
being created solely in an empty universe. Then to produce all
the vegetation before the sun and moon is clearly in reverse
order. J was obviously not scientifically orientated, but rather
highly imaginative in the use of his material, gathered from
earlier sources.

The 'Beginning' is all conjecture and mythical compared with
the latest scientific calculations, based on factual evidence.
Scientists state that the 'Atomic Clock' puts the formation of
the world at 4.5 billion years. The potassium argon test dates
the first humans at about 2.4 million years ago. Geologists
consider our earth to be several million years old. Leading

scientists put forward the 'Big Bang' theory that our planet came into existence suddenly and speedily, as it were 'in a flash' of great heat, providing the energy needed to produce matter from which eventually came man. That seems somewhat in agreement with the Biblical version of the Creation, however problematic appears its myth-like description. But there is no evidence to support this ancient Hebrew projection of seven stages of evolution as promulgated in the Bible. Nor whether life began simultaneously on other planets under the same Creator, or each with its own Big Bang, as scientists theorise. Nor indeed whether there was this envisaged Creator of anthropomorphic form, or a Supreme Spirit over all, directing Yahweh, and other gods in their duties and responsibilities – with Yahweh to create our world and all therein, including mankind.

There are many problems still unsolved especially the mysteries of Time, Space and the so-called laws of nature. Why did it take literally many thousands of years before the possibility arose of a single God, who was above all other gods in shape or form, unlike those who had previously been worshipped? Was Yahweh the complete invention of the unknown nameless scribe J, or did J's own studies of ancient and past history lead him to the belief (eagerly accepted and followed by his successors), in such a sole Supreme monotheistic God? This may well have been J's greatest contribution to world religion, led by the Jews, who still affirm, above all, the sole God: 'Hear O Israel, the Lord our God, the Lord is One'.

Thousands of clay tablets discovered from the first cuneiform scripts circa 3500 BC made by the Sumerians (who, like their ancestors still worshipped many gods of nature), and later by the Persians, Babylonians, Ellamites and the Phoenicians – all allude to the Beginning, but never to any sole god above all

2

others, except possibly Marduk, King of gods of Uruk. Yet those keen navigators, the Phoenicians, must have visited many distant lands and learnt of their gods and forms of worship. They too developed their own alphabet, from the Hebrew which also became the foundation of the Greek, hence must have kept records, as did the Sumerians. The Egyptians had many gods (including their own Pharaohs), mainly of sun and animals. Seemingly, in all that time, from primitive humans to the first Hibarus, there was no single God worshipped above all others.

So why did everything have to wait until the 10th century BC before there was any mention of a sole God? J's Yahweh warns his human creatures specifically not to worship other gods. He becomes demonstrably angry when they disobey, and seek other gods in the form of 'graven images', who do not answer back nor punish severely, and may give comfort, whereas Yahweh metes out harsh punishment for the slightest disobedience. All must accept his supremacy without demur.

Writing did not exist in those ancient times, so there is no recorded evidence to support any claims or theories. Only the tales and folklore passed down by oral transmission, and the pictorial evidence of our primitive ancestors on caves and rocks. Such original tales would become garbled and changed in substance, form and content, over the long period before the first written versions. To that first author we owe the 'Beginning' as first construed, though later changed again and again from the original, to suit the different taste and motives of later 'priestly' scribes.

The first forms of writing have been traced as far back as about 3500 BC. Early script cuneiform was impressed on tablets of river clay with sharpened wedge-shaped reeds, by those clever, advanced Sumerians, who dwelt between the

Tigris and Euphrates in the rich land of Mesopotamia. They are believed to have invented the wheel and the plough and money. Perhaps their greatest claim to fame was as the birthplace of Abram, who lived with his father Terah, and married Sarai, in Ur of the Chaldees, land of the magicians.

The Sumerian invention of over 100 different symbols was copied by their Semitic neighbours, Akkadians, Babylonians, Assyrians and later also the Phoenicians. This sign language baffled later generations until Major Rawlinson, whose hobby was deciphering ancient scripts, skilfully climbed the hazardous, steep face of the giant rock of Bisutun. He copied and then decoded the message, inscribed in three languages by Darius of Persia c 500 BC, by counting sign repetitions, and assigning them to the principal letters of our alphabet – a major ploy of decryption. But there was no reference to one particular God.

Later, the Sumerians were able to reduce their signs to about 24 characters. The Hebrews and Egyptians similarly developed their own forms of writing, including hieroglyphics. The Hebrews invented the first real alphabet about 3250 BC, with 22 letters but no vowels, copied by the Phoenicians and the Greeks. The Aramaic people, including the Phoenicians, settled in Syria c 1100 BC, as traders. Aramaic spread through Assyria, replacing cuneiform script. The Arabic script of Islam developed from Aramaic c 500 AD.

It is claimed by some that Moses wrote the Pentateuch. But there is no evidence, no record nor mention that Moses or Aaron ever wrote anything, difficult though this may be to comprehend. Even the stone tablets of the Law were inscribed on Mt. Sinai by Yahweh. Not a single tablet or scroll has surfaced, written with their experiences, during those forty years in the Wilderness, although Numbers 33:2 states: 'And

4

Moses wrote their goings forth, stage by stage'. None has ever been discovered, but is it possible that J may have had sight of some? He never reveals nor indicates any of his sources, to cast doubt on his originality. Moses, supposed to have been brought up as an Egyptian prince, would have found writing left to the priests, with their secret hieratic sacred script. Aaron, brother of Moses, had to be called to act as his mouthpiece, because he stuttered in his earlier years. No records, tablets or diaries have ever been discovered. So these Exodus years c 1260 are veiled in mystery, whilst Sumerians and others were quite prolific in their earlier tablet production and use in everyday life and general and household affairs, including mathematics and accounting.

No written records are extant from Abraham and the Patriarchs, so their years from c 2200 BC are all mystery and conjecture, without the expected written expressions of priestly wisdom and instructions, which did not obtain in their time. It was not until the 10th century BC, that an unknown, unnamed, but obviously well-educated person at the Court of Solomon's son, King Rehoboam of Judah, about 920 BC, wrote his own version of the Beginning. Fortunately, many fragments of his writings (on papyrus with a reed pen), have been discovered and translated from ancient Hebrew. This unknown author produced the first original biblical records.

He has become known as J, possibly because he was of the tribe of Judah. Whence he came or what his history or background, nothing is known. Happily for us J was no ordinary man, though obviously no scientist. He was, astonishingly, a writer of genius. As we come to know him from those parts of his writings discovered in the 19th century, we begin to realise how fortunate we are to encounter an author of such outstanding talent. Head and shoulders above all the later biblical writers, he has been likened to the Jewish Shakespeare, emerging from ancient history as an absolute original. Apparently there were no earlier valid Hebrew records for him to consult, only those clay tablets of Sumerians, Persians, Assyrians and many others, who all worshipped their many gods of nature and animals, as did the Egyptians. J had to trace oral traditional folklore, whether of myths, tales, sagas, domestic events or magic. These were centred on mankind, animals, the elements and all that concerned their daily lives, with stories, fantasies and legends, woven around their customs and habits, and especially nature, with which they were most concerned.

We know that early, primitive mankind worshipped the Sun, Light and Nature. These were their first and lasting gods. Fire was a form of magic associated with the heat of the Sun. But how and when such primitive faiths and beliefs gradually developed into other forms and gods remains a mystery. They undoubtedly exerted a great influence on their descendants. The ancient Hebrews, and later even the Israelites, fell under the influence of these 'foreign gods', incurring the wrath and vengeance of Yahweh. Laban, Jacob's father-in-law, treasured his household gods as did other Israelites. Seemingly Yahweh knew and accepted this 'begrudgingly', as long as he came first: 'Above all other gods'. Over all, however, was a Supreme Spirit Elyôn who assigned gods their duties: thus Yahweh was chosen to create and guide mankind.

Therefore we owe our first real knowledge and experience of them to J, and his research into oral tales and traditions, in his even earlier writings, of which but few fragments have been discovered. Our main concern is the Beginning and how far, if at all, we may accept J's wonderful stories as the true version. Or should we only acclaim him as the great author he undoubtedly was, who wove together all the information and folklore inherited from the past, into a glorious kaleidoscope of imaginary developments of the early stages of the Hebrews, who became Israelites, and first worshipped a spirit God called El?

But all matter in early times was imbued with spirit – every natural phenomenon was personified with its own El or spirit for guidance and protection; gods of the home, family personal gods and spirits of their dead ancestors. Demons haunted the night. The great god Tammuz was lord of vegetation, and the raising of seedlings, who died and rose again to be worshipped in wonder. Ritual was conducted at the growing of the crops, such as barley. Their storm god was in the shape of a wild bull, who later became Baal, also the begetter of life. God of fertility, he impregnated the earth with rain – a fierce unpredictable god, feared and worshipped with sacrifices. Others included Ashnan the grain goddess and Astarte, goddess of fruitfulness, and consort of Baal, all gods of nature and fertility. Ishtar was the principal goddess of love and war, who became Greek goddess Venus.

The Kenites of Sinai area descended from Cain and naturally worshipped J's god Yahweh. Moses merged Yahweh with El of Abram, and transformed El into the all-powerful universal deity of later ages, as the people changed and developed. Moses was the catalyst. But there are no records of priestly wisdom until hundreds of years after J. Priests began under Moses in the Wilderness. When he divided up the tribes according to Jacob's sons, he separated his own tribe of Levi to become the Priests, with Aaron his brother as leader. Priests soon developed their own special position of power and influence over the people, and even over the kings.

Surely Abram, brought up and educated with Sumerians, must have learned to read and write. Yet neither tablets nor records have been discovered. All we know we owe to others, without

7

his personal evidence or that of his family and descendants. So everything points to J as the unique, original author who put together all that is as yet known of these earliest years from Adam to Noah. With strong suspicion that much of it will have sprung from J's interpretation of early folklore, with his own discoveries, studies, observation and beliefs from within the Court at Jerusalem, with available records of the past to hand. Yet not a single tablet or scroll has been found. Were they destroyed, or did they ever exist?

However much we may enjoy his myths and fables in his own imaginative interpretation of the Beginning, the biggest problem of all is J's God Yahweh. If he did not inherit him in some form from earlier religions or forms of worship, whence did he come? There is no previous record of a single supreme God – or did J have recourse to knowledge of some unrevealed source as indicated at the end of Deuteronomy? Whether he actually believed it all himself, is open to doubt. J seems to have gloried in the thrill of knowing he was producing an original major work, encompassing all he could muster of the past history of his people, with all those ancient epic tales of the conduct and behaviour of mankind, with its mix of good and bad. Also the forms of worship and belief (including superstition and magic rather than spiritual), and adding his own inspiration and invention, to produce his undoubted masterpiece. Oral accounts would be memorised and passed on far more accurately than modern complex machinery age.

J's original opening passage in *Book of J* reads:

'Before a plant of the field was in earth, before a grain of the field sprouted, Yahweh had not spilled rain on the earth, nor was there man to work the land, yet from the day Yahweh made earth and sky, a mist from within would rise to moisten the surface.'

8

Compare J's poetic passage with later writers' prosaic version. They would not accept J's complete version, and many changes and amendments and alterations were made, before the final form of the Pentateuch was specified some 500 years later by the Redactor (Ezra). He chose his composite version from a comprehensive mixture and selection of all the previous writers' work. But, himself an Aaronite priest, he did not totally accept layman J's version, and inserted texts of other priestly writers, which changed the meaning. We are left still to wonder about J's original text. What means BEFORE and what is the significance of this mist rising from the earth, and allowing red clay to be shaped into Adam? Something is lacking in the text. J wrote accounts of situations before the opening chapters of the Bible, but though they would be of paramount interest, scarcely any have been found. However, many parts of his story of Genesis, Exodus and Numbers have been discovered, including his opening chapters, which were changed and altered by later priestly writers.

Professors H. Bloom and D. Rosenberg in their outstanding *Book of J*, quote from his original writings as transcribed:

'Yahweh shaped an earthling from clay of this earth and blew into his nostrils the wind of life.
Now look: man becomes a creature of the flesh.'

'As you sow, the sweat of your face, so you will reap your bread, till you return to earth – from it you were taken. Dust you are, só dust you return.'

Can there be any doubt as to the supreme literary talent and poetic inspiration of this, surely the original founder of the universal religion, from which was born not only Judaism, but also Christianity and Islam. If only J's writings had all been preserved in their original format, there might well be more

9

revealed of his principal sources. Yet the question still remains as to how much was due to his vivid imagination and undoubted literary skill. Further examples of his source material will be revealed later.

J was not writing for all the people, still largely uneducated and relying on oral transmission, but for those with adequate education and ability to read and grasp the challenging nature of his work and depth of thought, in those troublesome times in which he lived – embracing the development of religion, but principally his main historical characters and movements. As to whether we now should accept J's version (originally written in one seamless, continuous epic), remains to be discussed, debated and analysed, but never fully agreed, for the factual evidence required for proof does not yet exist.

We are left to decide for ourselves from our grasp of the original writings and any hidden meanings, what we may accept as possible or probable truth, in the knowledge that the Bible, which finally emerged from other priestly sources which took issue with J, bore little resemblance in many parts, to his version. We must seek to separate the ancient folklore, superstitions and tales of magic and mysticism woven together by the inspirational and imaginative mind of J, the greatest original Jewish writer, philosopher, poet and historian of his world, from any more acceptable version, if the truth can be deduced. The world's greatest writers who followed him through the centuries, often unknowingly pay tribute in their works, owing much of their inspiration to this anonymous author who emerged from the 10th century BC, to cause so much controversy, which has since burned steadily through so many thousands of years, and even now still poses unanswerable questions.

How many of his successors have removed parts of his scripts, altered or drastically changed them to suit their own ends and ambitions, especially the groups of priestly writers known as P (for priests)? These priests have even fought among themselves for supremacy between the two camps, following either Moses or Aaron. How many later successors through the centuries have pillaged, tortured, maimed and murdered in the name of religion? Fanatics are still prepared to torture and kill for their extremist faith. In fact, religion has caused more wars and conflicts, assassinations, inquisitions, fanatics' bombs and torture, making pariahs and outcasts, even of their own kith and kin, than any other source of 'man's inhumanity to man'.

The Bible, as we now know it, is of much different form and content from J's original work. Let us therefore attempt to follow, as best possible, the original work of J, and then compare it with efforts of other, much later, writers. Whatever our own personal beliefs or opinions, we all have much to learn from this early ancestor, who was seemingly too modest even to sign his name and give his own personal details. We must first accept that religion *per se* is really a legacy from our primitive ancestors, from humanoids to humans in more recognisable form.

They emerged into history as crude hunters and gatherers of food for survival, to form groups for family protection, a first animal instinct. They made enclosures within their boundaries which they defended, whilst learning to respect others' areas. Thus grew an order of social preference, with natural leaders and fierce fighters, as also those who planted the seeds, cared for domestic animals, gathered the crops and maintained the homes. In fact a microcosm, however primitive, of our own later development. The magical power of fire for cooking, warmth, shaping tools and weapons and keeping off wild animals and intruders, became a prime god, worthy with the sun, moon, light and fertility, of fear, obeisance and song and

11

dance in praise. Also sacrifice and gifts to appease. They had no priests, but relied on their leaders for guidance and control, esteeming them as priests in Sumer or even as gods in Egypt.

The Chaldean *Epic of Creation* recounts the world's beginnings and the building of Babylon under the protection of its god Marduk. It was like a sacred book, from the beginning of time:

'When the skies above were not named
Nor earth below pronounced by name'

In the myth of Atrahasis the gods become noisy and ill-behaved. So Ea and his wife Damkina create Marduk, the superior King of the gods. He performs a miracle:

'Let me put blood together and make bones too,
Let me set up primeval man: Man shall be his name'

So man is created to do the work of the gods, who may now rest in leisure. Is Marduk a prototype for Yahweh?

A similar Akkadian myth has Atrahasis (precursor of Noah) a dignified character. Belet-ili, the goddess of fertility, creates mortals (seven male and seven female) to do the labour of the gods. They grow too fast and troublesome, so she decides on a Flood to remove them. Erki warns Atrahasis, instructing him to build a boat and thus be saved.

These heroes of the earlier myths are all brave, handsome, honourable people, usually of miraculous birth with divine fathers or mothers, as in hero Gilgamesh. The most important gods of these early myths were Anu, the sky god of Sumeria; Ishtar (Sumerian Ianna), goddess of love and war; Ea, chief of the Apsu, sweet water under earth; Marduk, son of Ea, became king of the gods in Babylon; Shamash (Sumerian Utu), the great Sun god, judge of heaven and earth; Adad, weather god who controlled storms and rain with his Bull which bellowed like thunder and flashed lightning with his hooves; Ereshkigal, queen of the underworld, and Nanna, the moon goddess.

They were all concerned with mankind but not sympathetic, finding use for them to suit their own needs, and ever-demanding without respect or kindness. It was from these and other earlier myths, sagas and epics that J drew his research material for his monotheistic Yahweh, who was to be far above and superior to these ancient gods whilst sharing many of their characteristics. Hence his fierce, demanding and arbitrary nature and attitude to his creatures. Unfortunately Ur was attacked and burnt to ruins after Abram left, and Akkad in Northern Sumeria disappeared, but left its wonderful stories preserved in tablet form.

But J in the 10th century had witnessed the bitter humiliation of the destruction of David's great empire, through the fall from grace of Solomon and the splitting of his kingdom by his own failure to educate his sons. J must have witnessed the ruin of Jeroboam's ill-fated choice of territory with the capture and exile of his ten tribes of his kingdom of Israel, and wondered how long little Judah could hold out against the violent, brutal Assyrians and others crowding in for the kill of wounded Jerusalem. So his Yahweh may well have been his own fierce reaction to the ongoing collapse of that mighty empire of King David. Against this background was his story written, the story of his people who fought their way from Creation under their heroic leaders, sustained and forced forward by his mighty, warlike Yahweh, superior to all other gods in his strength and determination.

J did not view his god, whom he named Yahweh (from YHVH, without vowels, meaning 'Praise be to God'), as a

13

remote supreme deity, way above and beyond sight or scope of human concept. His Yahweh is a man-made God of nature similar to humans: 'Let us make man in our own image, after our likeness' (Genesis 1:26). So his Yahweh was in close relationship with man and had many of his characteristics. He was certainly not aloof, for he walked and talked with Adam and Eve, with Abram and Moses. But he also demanded, from the outset, strict obedience and unswerving loyalty from mankind, and was not prepared to suffer or forgive their inborn, natural deficiencies, but meted out severe instantaneous punishments.

J interpreted literally 'in our own image', as he reflects some of these same characteristics of mankind in Yahweh their Creator. He has many of their own traits: temperamental, ever-demanding, hasty-tempered, quick to anger and given to harsh punishment on instant decision, without reflection or consideration. He is often so irritated by the errant ill-behaviour and waywardness of his 'Children of Israel', that he is prepared not just to bully and browbeat them into order, but to condemn and even kill them for disloyalty and disobedience.

At first Yahweh is delighted and content with his Creation. But these human creatures soon cause trouble. He has provided an earthly paradise, the Garden of Eden, for his first-born Adam and Eve. When they disobey his only command, not to eat the fruit of the Tree of Knowledge, seeking equal power with him, they become the first to bear the severe punishment meted out by Yahweh to those who disobey him. There is to be no second chance, no 'punishment to fit the crime'. They are immediately expelled from their unappreciated paradise. Worst of all, they are eternally condemned, with all their descendants, for ever to labour by the sweat of their brow, to dig the hard earth to earn their

14

living. The serpent must slide on his belly for evermore, as enemy of mankind. Cherubs are sent out with flaming swords to guard his precious Tree of Knowledge and the Garden of Eden. What a terrible punishment! And why the necessity to keep his human creatures in sublime ignorance for ever? What then did he expect of them? Just to be his innocent playthings?

Genesis 5:2 says: 'male and female created he them, and blessed them, and called *their* name Adam, in the day when they were created'. The Talmudic and Persian forms of Creation myth represent God as first making a two-sexed being, a male and female joined together and then divided. That seems a quite different concept. In Genesis 1:27: 'And God created man in his own image, in the image of God created He them, male and female created He them'.

The legend of Paradise appears in all folklore – Egypt, India, Tibet, Babylonia, Persia, Greece, Mexico, with forbidden trees and serpents or dragons to steal immortality from man. The basic thought is that sex and knowledge destroy innocence and happiness, and are the origin of evil. Yet Genesis 1:23 says: 'And God blessed them; and God said unto them, be fruitful and multiply'. Seems a contradiction, but Ecclesiastes mourns likewise the loss of innocence. How then was mankind to survive? Possibly, woman was the lovely or evil agent of the serpent (or the devil). But J regarded women much more highly and portrayed their importance and dynamic resolution. He is more concerned with portrayal of characters rather than religion on his world stage, as he brings them clearly to life before us.

Now more fantasy interposes. The original image of one Adam and one Eve questions the possibility of propagation when, of their first born sons, Cain kills his brother for no viable reason. Cain is then expelled by Yahweh and forced into the wild as a sinner. Do we then trace our descent from this bloodstained survivor, who nevertheless, apparently succeeds in marrying and founding a city and people of his own? Some punishment for fratricide! But where could he possibly find a wife? Adam was the only man in the world to give birth to woman once, and only once. It was only later that their son Seth was born to take the place of Abel. Then they produced more sons and daughters who must have intermarried to propagate further. Maybe his long family history of begats was to persuade us of the truth of his vast panorama.

J seems so occupied with relating the emergence of mankind fully formed, that he forgets the normal state of human development in creating his further characters. Yet all later writers accepted J's imaginative concept of Adam and Eve, and faithfully included it in their versions. It was too good to change, and their imagination could not stretch to anything different, though they were ready to change much else to suit themselves in their rival priestly connivance, especially regarding Yahweh. This problem of propagation still remains unsolved in our present Bible, against all accepted rules of conduct and moral ethics.

Certainly J's Yahweh is unique among all previous gods. J was actually living in the quickening growth and development of the Jewish nation. His King Rehoboam, grandson of David, held court in David's sacred city of Jerusalem. His tribe of Judah and all the other tribes of Israel worshipped the same monotheistic God of Abraham, Isaac and Jacob, and followed the Laws of Moses, and the tenets of their accepted religion, in which they were all united. But we still have no written proof beyond J's authentic, original authorship. J does not indicate, nor refer to any sources from which he drew his Yahweh. We do not even know and cannot surmise why J put

16

together the letters YHVH from the ancient Hebrew alphabet, already in existence. So much is still missing, and so earnestly needed of early Hebrew writing, to guide us into their true history and development over those all-important years. There must surely be other tablets or scrolls yet to be found to fit together some of these pieces, to reveal the truth to our eager questioning. We cannot be expected to take everything for granted as the literal truth, without some real evidence or proof. Surely there must be quantities of those ancient scrolls, safely hidden and waiting to be discovered to reveal the truth of those all-important early years.

We do know that the later all-priestly writers of the five Books were not prepared to accept without question J's version of his anthropomorphic God Yahweh, so similar to man in his behaviour and reactions. Yet so demanding and domineering in his attitude. Quick to wrath and drastic punishment even without warning, showing no mercy to the sinners. Such a tough, harsh, unyielding and unforgiving Yahweh. But the priests wanted a deity to suit their own design, divorced from personal contact with mankind, issuing his edicts from way above, only through them, unseen, changed and modified.

Their Yahweh thus gave more power to the subjective desires of the priests, who were quite capable of almost taking his place. Certainly they claimed to be acting and interpreting for Yahweh, in warning the people as to their conduct. Prophesying doom, death and disaster should they disobey Moses' Laws, or fail to pay their due tithes to the Levite priests and bring them their sacrifices and harvest gifts – still continued in churches even now, though in more modified form. So we shall trace the changes in Yahweh, from the original J version to the altered priestly rendering over many hundred years, with the rapidly enhanced position of those power – and

17

position – hungry Aaronite priests, who sought to be accepted by all alike as Yahweh's deputies – to be themselves severely castigated by Jeremiah and other prophets.

Returning to the Beginning when the word was with J, what are we now to believe from the passage of time in Genesis from Adam to Noah? It is surmised that those first chapters, concluding with the amazing adventures of Noah and family and the epic of Babel, were products of J's vivid imagination, arising from all the folklore he had gathered from the past. For there were undoubtedly great, even gigantic floods featured similarly in many other countries, neighbouring and even far distant, in Africa and the East, to America. These still continue, and I personally witnessed and took part in the rescue of people trapped in the very tops of trees by the huge floods in India in 1942. The previous epic of Gilgamesh almost mirrors Noah's Flood, in company with many similar stories, almost universally portrayed.

J's Yahweh is hard and implacable. One could perhaps conjecture that Yahweh's dissatisfaction with the ill-conduct and transgressions of the humans in his otherwise satisfactory Creation, reflects J's own unhappiness with the deteriorating state of his own generation. Split asunder, Israel and Judah seem both beset from enemies within, as also without. Solomon's sons failed to carry on the great empire built by David and their father, who failed to educate them in their duties.

J was no ordinary man. To his perception, deep research and knowledge of the distant past, his ancestors and their mode of life and customs, we owe our combined religious faiths and our inherited laws and customs. So it behoves us to examine more closely all that he accomplished, his possible motives, and what transpired after him. Above all, his Yahweh is of

18

the utmost importance. He envisages this Supreme Being as close to his Creation. His power flows with complete and immediate certainty, to create the world in the forms he decides and in his chosen order. This is not so different from our scientists' 'Big Bang' theory of the instant birth of our planet – which, nevertheless, could not have come into instantaneous existence, fully grown and complete, with sky, heaven and earth, vegetation, animals and finally humans. How do scientists account for all that immediate growth, whether of seven days, seven months or years? They now calculate over 4.2 billion years of ongoing slow development, with humans emerging last of all, almost as an extra animal development.

Yahweh is faced with a void, which must now be filled. So the basic elements of the firmament, earth and water, are duly assembled. The earth is bare, so has to be given life and growth of all manner of vegetation, animals, birds and insects. Finally, and only after all else is satisfactorily created, is humankind considered. Not of such high value as to come before all the animals. Indeed man is almost an afterthought, scooped out of the red clay and fashioned into shape similar to Yahweh himself. All done within the allegorical seven days of J's concept of the Creation, certainly more imaginatively poetic than reasoned scientific – owing much to similar material from previous versions of neighbouring countries and scribes.

For J, his Yahweh is in close relationship with man, who is 'in his image'. A God not remote, distant, unseen, but in immediate contact and close control, seeking harmony with his human creatures, as he has already established with his animals. Yahweh obviously placed woman on a higher plane than man. Eve was not made like Adam from common clay. She was taken from Adam's rib and part of his body. This is of profound significance. Not only was this the first and only

19

time that man gave birth, Eve was seemingly intended to be of higher order than her earthy husband.

These first humans were treated like demi-gods, with their own paradise, made specially for them to live an idyllic life of unadulterated pleasure without work, stress or strain. But Yahweh allowed them to have brains, senses, imagination and above all, free will and innate human curiosity. If he had not wished them to try the fruit of the Tree of Knowledge, why go to the trouble of planting these two trees of Life and Knowledge in the middle of the Garden, to arouse their curiosity? In addition we have talking animals, with the serpent acting as tempter to the woman's inquiring mind. He is condemned not to extinction but to his future rôle as the devil. But why so empower the devil's advocate, when Yahweh himself is supposed to foster and guide his human creation?

Now a far worse fate awaits them. Complete banishment from their idyllic paradise is surely punishment enough. Worse still – condemned to struggle hard for ever for their sustenance 'by the sweat of their brow', they now start the human race on its eternal path of suffering, birth, lifelong toil and death awaiting. 'Dust to dust' with no promise or condition of amelioration. What a terrible punishment for the whole human race, meted out by a harsh, unforgiving Yahweh, for just one slip in their erstwhile perfect behaviour!

Yahweh is to meet much worse conduct from their successors. They have not long to wait before the stark nature of their future lives is brought home to them. Their rough hunter son Cain kills gentle shepherd brother Abel in a fit of jealousy. So murder, death and exile waste no time in bringing tragedy to them in all its harsh severity. What of the following writer E's strange, unbelievable miscegenation, unearthly story of the Sons of God pursuing 'earthly maidens' and producing giants, reminiscent of the promiscuous behaviour of the Greek gods, who may owe their derivation to this astonishing tale, possibly adapted from an earlier Hittite account of forbidden dalliance of their gods. And what of Eve who refutes the rôle of Adam in the birth of Cain, their first-born: 'I have begotten a man with the aid of the Lord'. Hints of the Church's obliteration of Joseph, Mary's husband, or the engendering of Sarai's birth of Isaac without Abraham, then over 100 years old.

J's opening story of human experience is striking in its stark reality. The contrast between past, present and future for the first humans is painted in darkest colours by our scribe. However allegorical, this skilful storyteller J leaves us in no doubt that he was fully aware of the tragic situation of mankind. He also had the advantage of watching history unfold from the comparative security of Rehoboam's Court, witnessing the deterioration of David's great Empire. Yet he shows us that life must go on, whatever the current personal situation, and the unending problems besetting our world. He produces a rich variety of colourful characters with all their personal adventures and experiences. Also the effect upon each other of the leaders and followers, the strong and the weak, in peace and in war. He is not only a wonderful story-teller, but has sharp wit and a biting sense of humour (as we shall see with Noah and Babel), which often helps to alleviate some of his most tragic scenes. This Prologue really ends with the outrageous story of the drunken Noah, and Yahweh's mischievous interference with the building of the Tower of Babel, to alleviate the awful dismay of learning that Yahweh cannot any longer bear the sight and sound of all his first generations of mankind.

Without hesitation he decides to remove them all, lock, stock and barrel – the whole of his Creation (which he first found so good), in one major action, 'for it repenteth Me that I have made them' (Genesis 6:7). Yahweh visits the one good, trust-worthy man left, Noah, grandson of Methuselah, to detail the operation. Noah is given explicit instructions to build this huge boat of gopher wood (cypress), with room to house not only Noah, wife and family, but seven sets of all 'clean' (sacrificial) animals, birds and insects and fishes, and one set each of 'unclean' (P will differ sharply). All to be housed, watered and fed in this great Ark-shaped vessel. There they must all remain, sealed inside by Yahweh, whilst for 40 days the rains pour down and the water level rises, until all else on earth is completely drowned. As long as it takes for Yahweh to wreak his wrath and vengeance on all his Creation, for the innocent animals are to die with the guilty people, men, women and children and all else on the earth.

We are left wondering what manner of Yahweh is this to destroy his own Creation so wilfully, and what size vessel would really be needed to house all these selected animals? And yet, he still preserves a selection of all animals, birds, insects, to start again after the Flood. Curious conduct for a Yahweh supposedly determined to drown all mankind and all his Creation, which he originally found so good. After all this high drama, comes the discovery of previous similar antique Flood stories, sagas and dramas to be found in other countries' records, questioning the authenticity of J's scenario which was certainly neither unique nor original.

Picture Noah with his sons Shem, Ham and Japhet (Shem lived to over 500 years and begat the Semites from whom we are descended), cutting and shaping the gopher wood to build this massive craft to Yahweh's design. What must have been their thoughts and comments as they hammered away, shaping the wood and caulking and sealing it with pitch and bitumen? What would their wives and families have had to say about this fantastic, huge operation, and why it had to be kept

22

secret – especially with curious neighbours' comments and questions? Even gathering all those animals, birds and insects together must have been in itself a mighty task to be done in haste and secrecy. If only we might have a transcript of the neighbours' gossip and views on the Noah family's peculiar conduct! Certainly the Ark was not big enough to contain them all, with the food and water, for six weeks.

It is beyond our conjecture even to get all stowed finally aboard and the doors sealed by Yahweh. Then the rains pouring down and the waters steadily rising, bearing the bodies and remains of all the earth's contents floating past their windows! Forty days and nights to endure, with all the ark's contents to maintain, must have been intolerable to bear, a task beyond Hercules. Surely Noah was entitled to celebrate with his first wines after it was all safely accomplished. At least he made his mark in history as the originator of the vine.

This comic aftermath breaks the tension, so heavily built up through this terrible story, so painstakingly recounted by J in all its ghastly details. One feels sorry for poor old Noah after all the strain he suffered. But also for innocent son Ham who happened to find his father lying exposed in a drunken stupor as a result of his wine-bibbing. What an accomplished story-teller is J with his artistic twist in this grim tale. The cold-blooded murder of the universe by Yahweh, ending with an hilarious drunk scene, with waking Noah cursing the innocent son of Ham for supposedly daring to reveal the disgraceful self-exposure of his grandfather. The planting of the world's first vines and the strength of its first wine is J's comic opera interlude, before Yahweh's next attack on mankind.

J writes: 'Yahweh was moved: Never again will I judge the earth because of the earthling. Imagination bends his human heart to bad designs from the very start. Never again will I cut off all that lives, as I have done' (see Genesis 8:21-22).

But he breaks his promises and covenants again and again, for his hot temper pronounces instantaneous deadly judgement. Far worse would have happened with his hasty death wishes, had not Moses diplomatically steered him away. Nevertheless from Genesis to David, he continues to bring down on his 'chosen people', his 'Children of Israel', instantaneous death from flood and fire, pestilence and plague, sword and from battle within and without, even to opening the earth to have them swallowed up. He devises all manner of harsh punishments, including sickness and disease, but finally bringing down their enemies to defeat and destroy them without compunction.

Obviously this is a story culled from that ancient folklore which was J's inheritance, with all its myths and magical whimsy. Yet some still seem determined to accept as true Noah's story, with all its dreadful consequences. There is a constant search for Mount Ararat in Turkey, the believed site of the Ark's landing. Even law-suits pursued between learned explorers! Can one not see J quietly amused at all those determined to prove the Bible right in every detail? When it is so obviously one of his most imaginative stories, culled from many similar flood legends. The claim is even made of discovery of a 'boat-shaped geological formation' south of Mount Ararat, the very length of Noah's boat, 300 cubits (about 500 feet). Opposition claims it to be simply a fold of a 110-year-old sea bed. Similar claims have been made over the years. But the nearest scientific findings seem to bear out nature producing giant floods in those ancient times, just as she continues to do even now.

Cuneiform tablets unearthed by British archaeologist George

24

Smith in King Ashurbaipal's library at Nineveh, gave the Akkadian version of Gilgamesh and the Babylonian Noah, called *Ut-napishtin*. Also the ancient Sumerian story of Ziusudra (the 'long-lived'), who was ordered to build an ark. He finished up after his Flood in the Paradise land of Dilmun – supposedly Bahrein. The *Egyptian Book of the Dead* has its story of the Flood, as have many other countries from Iceland and India to America and Mexico.

Whoever could believe that J's Yahweh, harsh though his punishments were normally, could wipe out all mankind and all the rest of his Creation in one fell swoop, leaving poor old Noah to bear the brunt, and then have to refurbish the world? A task which Hercules and all the Greek Gods could not accomplish. But Homer, classic storyteller, would not have dared cross swords with J in his breathtaking fables. J has the more personal style and approach. For J is still not finishing his amazing Prologue until he inserts, before the end of Noah and his necessarily long-stretching family, his final unique world-gripping story of the Tower of Babel, a story still told and retold. Here is the authentic J, from Professor Rosenberg:

'Now listen, all the earth uses one tongue, all the same words. Watch – they journey from the East, arrive at a valley in the land of Sumer, settle there. "We can bring ourselves together," they said, "like stone on stone, use brick for stone, bake it hard. We can build a city and tower, its top touching the sky – to arrive at fame."

'Said Yahweh: "They are one people with the same tongue. They conceive this between them, and it leads up until no boundary exists to what they will touch. Between us let us descend, baffle their tongue until each is scatterbrain to his friend."

'From this Yahweh scattered them over the whole face of the earth, the city there came unbound. That is why they named the place Babel – their tongues baffled by Yahweh.'

Was there ever such a fantastic story, stretching our imagination with colourful word pictures to fill a whole volume, yet encompassed in a few telling lines? One must admire this tight little complete entity which succeeded in soaring above its biblical source, to be repeated for evermore. But why such rough usage of people who wanted to join together in one language and friendship? What was there to worry Yahweh about their unity? Perhaps the clue lies in his oft-repeated warning that he is a 'Jealous God'. Thus does J sign off his Prologue of fables, epics and folklore, before entering his really serious history of the Bible. For him, this encompassed what became known as Genesis, Exodus and Numbers, plus Leviticus and Deuteronomy. Whatever else he wrote has sadly never been discovered – as yet. But there is still hope with the wonderful work of our archaeologists and geologists.

Now comes the all-important entry of Abram ('exalted father'), living with Terah, his father and family in Ur of the Chaldees (land of the magicians). Seemingly unhappy with the customs and manifold gods of the Sumerians, Terah takes his family with Lot, his nephew, to return to Haran after smashing the false images. There they dwell and flourish in the centre of the main trade route between Egypt and Babylon. When Terah dies, Abram receives a call from Yahweh (Genesis 12:1-3) according to J:

'Bring yourself out of your birthplace, out of your father's house, your homeland – to a land I will bring you to see. I will make you a greatness, a nation and a blessing: of your name, fame, bliss is brought out of you. And I will bless

26

them that bless thee, and him that curses thee will I curse, and in thee shall all the families of the earth be blessed.'

Lot chose to go to the Jordan Valley and Sodom, where unfortunately the people had 'gone bad' and evil. Abram moved to Mamre, beside Hebron, to hear from Yahweh: 'Look now toward heaven and count the stars.... So will thy seed be' (Genesis 15:5). But later to receive the unpleasing prophecy: 'Know of a surety that thy seed shall be a stranger in a land that is not theirs and shall serve them; and they shall afflict them four hundred years;... and afterwards they shall come out with great substance.' (Genesis 15:13-14) Then in the next breath he offers as compensation: 'But thou shalt go to thy fathers in peace'. (Genesis 15:15). It is almost like sardonic humour to cause Abram terrible distress at this tragic future of his descendants, but then the throwaway line – 'but don't worry, you will have a peaceful death'. Another instance of J's creative imagination and wry sense of ironic humour. Yahweh is so unfeeling that he is insensitive to poor Abram's unhappy feelings of the future sufferings of his family and descendants.

Sarai, at 90 and barren, laughs to scorn Yahweh's messengers when she overhears them prophesying Abram a son. She has already presented her Egyptian maid Hagar to Abraham, who bears him a son, Ishmail. Hagar, expelled now by Sarai's jealousy, flees into the desert, to be found by Yahweh's angel at the watering hole near Shur. The angel comforts her: 'Your seed I will sow beyond a man's eye to count. Ishmail you shall name him. The tents of his rebellion will rise before the eyes of his brothers.' Hence the birth of the Arab nation (cf. Genesis 18:12-15). So Abraham has produced another great nation-to-be! 'Abraham will emerge a great nation, populous, until all nations of the earth see themselves blessed in him.' Here is J at his most solemn prophetic.

27

The original J: so within her Sarai's sides split: 'Now that I'm used to groaning, I'm to groan with pleasure? My Lord is also shrivelled.' 'Why is Sarai laughing?' asked Yahweh of Abram. 'Is a thing too surprising for Yahweh?' 'In the time a life ripens and appears I will appear to you and Sarai, a son.' Sarai hid her feeling: 'No, I wasn't laughing' – she had been scared. 'No,' he said now, 'your sides split, count on it.' Genesis 21:1: 'And the Lord visited Sarah as he had said, and the Lord did unto Sarah as he had spoken.' Can it be possible that it was Yahweh, 'the Lord', who engendered Isaac, a forecast of later events?

Lot's ill-chosen Sodom and Gomorrah become so steeped in sin that Yahweh once again decides on complete destruction. The Abraham who walks with him along the road to Sodom has matured from the early unquestioning servant. Now he actually dares to bargain with Yahweh in an attempt to save the cities. Not 50, not 45, not 20, will you settle for ten good people to save them? But his attempt fails, for Yahweh retorts that there are not even five good people to be found there. Judging by the reception given to Yahweh's messengers on their exploratory visit, only just saved by Lot, it is not surprising, for they were steeped in sin, in both cities.

So Lot and his family have to flee in great haste: 'Now Yahweh spilled on Sodom and Gomorrah, a volcanic rain; fire from the sky.'(J) Once again, total destruction. But his un-named wife, foolishly disobeying Yahweh's command, looks back to witness the horror and destruction and is turned into a pillar of salt, to be destroyed by the licking of animals. Stretching even J's imaginative powers. But similar tales are legion, arousing the imagination elsewhere. There is a Buddhist story of their wandering saint, refused entry to the city of Holaolakia by their evil people. They destroyed the whole city, saving only one man who offered hospitality.

There is even a tale of North Yorkshire, when two saints visited the sinful town of Simmerwater in Aysgarth, only to be rebuffed by the sinful people there. They destroyed the whole town, sparing only one poor cottager who bravely offered them care and hospitality.

Lot settled in a cave in the mountains. But his two daughters, angry because they have been robbed of husbands, cannot face the shame of infertility. They seduce their father, having made him drunk, to bear his illegal sons Moab ('from father'), and Ben Ami ('son of my kin'), who founded the Moabites and Ammonites, who will cause much future trouble for the Israelites. A truly tragic result of Yahweh's total extinction of Sodom and Gomorrah, with J in his darkest mood at this further revelation of Yahweh's powers of wholesale destruction.

Time passes and Isaac grows, needing a wife. So we have the entertaining story of Abraham, trusting only his distant kinsfolk, dispatching his servant to seek a suitable wife for Isaac among them. Hence the entrancing story of J's heroine Rebecca at the well. She so graciously receives the servant at Haran:

'For your camels I will pour too, until they have drunk enough.'

Her brother Laban, noting the gold nose ring and bracelets of gold gifts, is only too ready for such a wealthy marriage, greedy for his share of the settlement and dowry. We meet this crafty relative again with the next generation of this very human patriarchal family.

Abram is now nearing 100 and a staunch monotheist, thereby receiving Yahweh's blessing and promise that Canaan would become the entrance to the Promised Land for the future of his multitudinous descendants, to be 'numerous as the stars'. An offer he could not refuse. He now becomes Abraham, exalted 'Father of All Nations'. Jews, Christians and Muslims alike will all trace their ancestry back to Abraham. If only all were even now allied in this great relationship there might yet be peaceful harmony, so much to be desired in our troubled world.

Abraham, with his quiet way, was no great leader, but rather the faithful follower of Yahweh. He duly entered Canaan at Shechem peacefully, encountering no opposition and doing exactly as commanded. Whereas Moses was not even to be allowed to cross the boundary, despite his long years of hard toil and loyal leadership of all the Children of Israel. Clearly Yahweh had his favourites from Abram to David. One wonders whether Abraham was aware that Yahweh had already killed off one whole generation of his Creation, with whom he became so dissatisfied that he drowned the whole earth and its contents, except for Noah and his family and selected animals. If so, he may have questioned his own possible fate. The Yahweh who ordered the binding of Isaac for human sacrifice was the same God who will later attempt to murder Moses, for no apparent reason, as he sets out on his journey as commanded, back to Egypt, from which he had been forced to flee. We will later try to show the connection, as Yahweh seeks to test stringently all those to whom he entrusts his missions, and are forced to suffer for this 'honour', when bestowed upon them.

However, Abraham receives far gentler treatment, coaxed by Yahweh to leave his family inheritance in the safety of Haran. He ventures forth into the unknown in complete obedience, as he shows when prepared to sacrifice his only son Isaac, born in his old age, at the whim and connivance of Yahweh. Did

30

he not even wonder how he would have been able to face Sarah, his wife, become mother at 90, as murderer of their only son? He would surely have feared his reception from doughty Sarah, now over 100, at his destruction of her son, late-born at the instigation of Yahweh himself, now to be sacrificed for no valid reason, but just a whim. Her mocking laugh would change to bitter condemnation.

Much of J's original text of this period became rewritten by his successors, the priestly scribes who tried to soften his harsh delineation of Yahweh. But they failed to weaken J's firm portrayal of his main characters. J was so vibrant, clear and forthright – precise and economic with his words. He presents his humans stark and unadorned. Clearly he is imaginative, but not sentimental in the delineation of his characters. How much he actually believed, in what he wrote from his position within the Court of King Rehoboam, we can only surmise. But he was obviously part cynic and part humorist, with an ironic sense of humour which adds spice to his stories, and softens some of the tragic events he unfolds. Like all authors, he is prepared to use all previous information and material researched for the weaving of his own intricate web. His Yahweh undoubtedly sprang from the anthropomorphic gods of previous folklore, who often took human shape, emotions and manners, whilst retaining supernatural powers. Their behaviour was of similar nature to Yahweh and the source of J's astonishing Deity.

Isaac enjoys a happy, fruitful marriage to Rebecca and prospers. His greatest moment comes with the birth of the twin sons Esau and Jacob. But from then on his peaceful life is shattered. Jacob, ambitious even in the womb, cannot bear to allow Esau to emerge first and thus gain the right of inheritance of the first born son. He clutches Esau's heel as he emerges, hence his name Jacob, meaning 'heel clutcher'.

31

Yahweh appears to Rebecca saying:

'Two nations are in thy womb, and two peoples shall be separated from thy bowels, and the elder shall serve the younger' (Genesis 25:23) (so Jacob's future was already ordained).

Jacob was inordinately jealous of his brother, and is supported by his mother who prefers smooth, handsome Jacob to her rough, red-haired, inarticulate hunter and earthy son Esau. Jacob bides his time and catches Esau returning weary and hungry after a long day hunting. He is tempted by the smell of the stew his brother is preparing, but is refused sustenance until his hunger knows no bounds. When Jacob makes the condition of his inheritance for a 'mess of pottage', Esau foolishly accepts, seeing nothing specially worthwhile in his life.

So Jacob cheats him, and when Isaac is on his deathbed, plots with his mother also to trick his father. Rebecca has him wrap himself in animals' rough, hairy skins. Isaac, now almost blind, grasps him and is deceived into believing him to be Esau, despite some difference in voice, and gives him his blessing. So once again, cunning, ambitious Jacob has cheated his brother out of his inheritance and his father's blessing. Yet it is unbelievable that Isaac could be persuaded by such hurried, poorly disguised mummery into accepting smooth-voiced Jacob for his beloved Esau. Not the usual quality of J's scenes – a somewhat laboured, unconvincing story – but he is planning Jacob's future important rôle, whereas Esau is but a pawn in J's great game. There is a similar story in the *Epic of Gilgamesh* of the intense rivalry of twin brothers – undoubtedly known to J.

Now the time comes for Jacob to seek a wife. He falls deeply

32

in love with his cousin Laban's youngest daughter Rachel. Laban agrees to the marriage on condition that Jacob work seven years for her. Passionate Jacob agrees and valiantly works seven years. Then he is married, only to find that he in turn has been cheated. Cunning Laban, to get his elder daughter married first, as was the custom, covered her in veils so that Jacob, unable to see her, marries Leah. He is honour bound to live with her, and they have ten children, important for Israel's future, though apparently only six are from Leah, four others supplied per Rachel and Leah's handmaidens, to keep Jacob contented.

Jacob is still in love with Rachel and demands to wed her. Laban agrees on condition that Jacob work for him a further seven years, and Jacob has to accept. So, in his most romantic tale, J has Jacob prepared to work 14 years for his beloved Rachel. However, Rachel takes her revenge on this cheating father, who has made her lose her first bloom of romance to satisfy his selfish cunning. When they prepare to leave, she steals her father's most precious treasure, his household gods, and hides them under her saddle. Laban searches everywhere but dare not disturb Rachel, already pregnant, seated on her camel. So on to the next stage of the development of Jacob.

Jacob learns that his brother Esau is coming to meet him with 400 armed men, and likely seeking revenge. So he splits his family and entourage into two, sending them in different directions for safety. He is accosted by a stranger as, at the Ford of Jabbok, he stands alone, and has to wrestle for his life all night long, until dawn. Acknowledging defeat, Yahweh's angel damages his hip, making him limp for the rest of his life. But he names him no longer Jacob, the heel clutcher. He is now to be Israel (God clutcher). This place is now named Penu-el. 'For I came face to face with Elohim.' A momentous meeting, presaging the future of Israel.

33

Esau meets his brother, now Israel, obviously changed for the better. All is forgiven and the brothers find peace and harmony together. Such is J's most romantic story, unusual for J, who normally finds his pleasure in stronger tales, as will soon become evident.

Jacob fathers 12 sons whose names are of future importance in their people's history, to become leaders of the 12 tribes. He has six sons by Leah, then two from Leah's handmaiden. A further two from Rachel's handmaiden (to comfort him in her absence). Then finally Joseph and Benjamin with his beloved Rachel. On the whole, the two sisters looked after him very well. But they did not know they were producing the future 12 tribes of Israel, with their sons as the first princes and leaders.

Joseph, Rachel's son, is his father's favourite. But he is already relating strange dreams, in which he is always superior to his brothers, who grow to dislike him. They plot his death and whilst tending the sheep, they bind him and throw him into a deep well to die. Fortunately, some traders find him and, as a comely lad, sell him to the Egyptian, Potiphar. J now enjoys telling his fantastic creation of Joseph the dreamer's rise to glory. It is a well-constructed story, beginning with his brothers' attempt to murder him, rescue by traders who sell him to Egyptian Potiphar, who promotes him to overseer. Like the serpent in Eden, his wife tries to tempt Joseph who, as a good loyal servant to his master, refuses. Revengeful wife now convinces husband of supposed attempt on her by Joseph, who is immediately thrown into jail.

There is an almost identical previous Egyptian tale of brothers Anpu and Bata. Anpu's wife attempts to seduce Bata, who refuses. Incensed, she accuses him of infidelity. Bata flees for his life, but eventually convinces his brother, on oath, of the truth. Anpu then has his wife put to death. Later stories copied, like Phaedra and Hippolytus.

Again rescued, this time by Pharaoh's butler, convinced of Joseph's ability to explain the meaning of dreams, recommends Joseph to Pharaoh, who is troubled by fearful dreams, which none of his priests or magicians can explain. Joseph, released from prison, solves Pharaoh's dreams with his awesome prophesy of Egypt's future problems. The world-famous story of the seven fat years followed by seven lean years (how often repeated in truth and substance through the centuries), brings Joseph fame and promotion to Chief Steward and Pharaoh's trusted right-hand man. Reconciliation with his family follows, and Jacob is brought to greet his beloved son and live out his days contented in Goshen, where his family wax fruitful and wealthy. (Genesis 39:7-20)

Now comes the tragedy to wipe out all those good years under a benevolent Pharaoh. Later Pharaohs turned against the Hebrews, flourishing in Goshen, and put them under bondage of increasing severity. They were reduced to slave-state, brick-making and menial tasks for hundreds of years, lacking a saviour. Egyptian hieroglyphics tell the story of the enslavement of the Apiru c 1500 to 1200 BC. J now produces his next astonishing black story. Pharaoh, fearing the rapidly increasing Hebrews as a future powerful menace, now issues a decree to have all their infant sons killed. A family of the tribe of Levi plans to save their new-born son. His sister conceals him in a waterproof basket to be carried by the tide to the bathing place of the royal princess, who adopts him (similar stories will be discussed later).

There are many similar imaginative birth stories from other sources. The *Epic of Gilgamesh* tells how his mother, daughter of King Senechoros of Babylon, had a child by an unknown lover. Her guardian, fearing the king's anger, threw her from the castle parapet. An eagle swooped and caught her, depositing her in a garden. The gardener took her home and reared her.

King Sargon of Agadde (later Akkade) was deposited on the Euphrates in a wicker basket, to be rescued by the water-carrier. Brought up as a gardener, he obtained a post as cup-bearer to the King Kish and then rose to fame. As first Akkadian emperor, he conquered Sumeria in 2335 BC. King Cyrus of Persia was supposedly brought up by a herdsman.

Paris of Troy was left exposed to the wilds, to be rescued by a she-bear who took the babe to the Queen who adopted him.

So we are again in the world of fantasy, readily accepted in ancient times.

King Ur-Nammu (c 2100 BC) was first Leader of Sumeria, regaining power. He was, like the future Moses, a great leader of his people, in character and ability, founding a dynasty and building a big Ziggurat at Ur to Nanna, the Moon goddess. Quiet, determined and resourceful, he rescued and taught his Sumerian people.

But Prince Ra-Mose remains aware of his real family, and concerned about the dreadful conditions of his people under Pharaoh, Rameses II.

One day he witnesses a taskmaster cruelly beating a Hebrew, and kills him. He then must flee from the wrath of Pharaoh, who seeks to murder him. His only safety lies in the pitiless Sinai desert where, against all expectations, he continues to survive. At last he finds a well, but comes upon the scene of rough shepherds refusing to allow some young maidens to draw water for their sheep. Moses confronts the shepherds and sees them off. The grateful girls take him to their father Reuel, Midian priest and farmer, who offers him hospitality out of gratitude. Moses lives contentedly with Reuel, who gives him his daughter Zipporah in marriage, treats him as a member of his family and later becomes his adviser, as Jethro.

Now comes the call of Yahweh, from within a bush that is burning but not consumed by flames. After the introduction, Yahweh reveals his mission to Moses. Having at last become concerned at the tragic situation in which he has allowed his people, Yahweh is now determined on their release. Moses is chosen to confront Pharaoh and reveal that he is Yahweh's emissary, to demand release of all the Hebrews. Moses, a quiet, modest man, demurs. He is not fit for such an onerous task – and besides, he has speech difficulties. Yahweh brusquely brushes aside such excuses, saying he will provide Aaron, his brother, to help him. This is the first we hear of Aaron, and he somehow does not feature much more in Exodus until Sinai, where he has an important rôle.

Moses undertakes his commission and goes to take farewell of his family. But, for no acceptable reason, Yahweh suddenly decides to kill him – without any explanation or cause given. (What can J have had in mind in this strange twist in his tale?) Yahweh sends two messengers for this dreadful assassination. Zipporah, worried about Moses' departure on this strange mission, awakes to see the approaching menacing figures. She immediately divines their intent, and takes instantaneous action. With a sharp knife she circumcises her son Gershom, and then challenges these would-be assassins to take further blood. This is a fantastic story. Whether from the sight of the bloody operation, or brave Zipporah's menacing knife, they retreat. This is a tale that has baffled everybody, and there is seemingly no valid explanation of why Yahweh,

37

having chosen Moses for this momentous task, should suddenly seek to kill him. It remains a mystery, but we may offer a possible solution, of testing his chosen emissaries, to ensure their physical, mental and moral strength to carry through their mission.

We now learn of Moses, gathering strength and command, and bearding Pharaoh with a request to let the elders of his people go with him into the desert to pray and confer. Pharaoh makes his first refusal, to be followed by a series of plagues to bring begrudging acceptances, but always repudiated by 'hardening of his heart'. No matter how Moses uses Yahweh's remarkable ability to plague the Egyptians, nothing moves Pharaoh to change his mind permanently. Rameses II was a hard, brutal ruler, unlikely to be persuaded to release this great mass of useful slaves without strongest convincing.

Now comes the fateful manoeuvre by Yahweh. He will finally resort to the ploy used by Pharaoh himself, which introduced Moses to the story, saved from Pharaoh's murder squad by his sister and the princess. Moses is to warn all his people to stay firmly and securely bolted inside their houses that night, and not dare open to any. They are to mark their lintels clearly with blood of a fresh-killed lamb so that Yahweh's avenging angels will pass them by. Every first-born son of Egypt will be killed that night, including Pharaoh's heir, but the Israelites' sons will be passed over and all will be saved. So definite are Yahwehs' commands that Moses has to order preparations to be made for all to leave the very next day, with food to be cooked in haste, and bread without yeast or time to leaven.

Thus was the stage set of this most inspired scenario in the Old Testament. What a tremendous task for Moses, first to force Pharaoh to let them go, then marshal all his forces of over 600,000 men with all their women and children, carriages of any kind, to convey the sick and frail, cattle and poultry to be rounded up, so that the great Exodus march might begin with none left behind. But there still lay great problems ahead. They made for the narrowest crossing at the Sea of Reeds, but how to get them all safely across? J brings Yahweh back into a major role, first to slow down the Egyptian forces, ordered to the attack by recalcitrant Pharaoh (once again changing his mind), sending clouds of mist behind the escapees to blind their followers. Then fire to indicate the way to the spot on the river, where he will hold back the waves long enough for all to cross. Finally, to lure on the Egyptian chariots until, stuck in the mud in the midst of the river bed, the tide changes and the currents drown them all. There is no end to Yahweh's colourful executions.

Books, poems, songs, plays and films have been made of this fabulous epic tale. Once safely ashore, they now find themselves entering the dismal, lonely, desert wilderness at Succoth, a strange unwelcoming country, so that many think longingly already of their home in Goshen. Moses, now their acknowledged leader, must take command, whilst following instructions from Yahweh, whose declared intention it was to 'set my people free'. But this is a wearisome, hard, tough experience, if this is what freedom betokens. They are doomed to wander in this immense wasteland for 40 years. They are gradually being hardened and prepared to withstand its rigours, and become used to self-disciplines far different from the existence in Egypt. They will suffer untold hardships with constant hunger and thirst and other privations. Such relief as wild fruit, manna from the dew, do not make up for the lack of meat and vegetables. This is the strangest, most extraordinary epic tale of the Bible. No other similar or matching stories have ever been found.

Moses, now a more mature leader, divides them into tribes bearing the names of Jacob's sons, duly appointing them as leaders. His and Aaron's tribe of Levi will be the priests, led by Aaron, to worship Yahweh and keep the people to the general religious rules. How can one conjecture the terrible strain on Moses, trying to keep this unruly, mixed-up mass of all ages in order, to maintain their daily sustenance, and keep alive the hope of reaching the Promised Land. They are now dubbed 'Children of Israel', an apt title for this great crowd of mixed generations, suddenly released from hundreds of years of bondage under hard taskmasters, into the comparative freedom of movement without fear of whiplash. But they could not easily grow accustomed to this new self-discipline and rigorous mode of living, imposed on all alike. They were often like fractious children, errant, resentful, even hysterical at times, quarrelling and aggressive and ever demanding of their leader Moses, who had to bear the brunt of it all.

Forty years seems an interminably long time, but they did not know this at the outset, and certainly needed hard training to be welded into a composite whole, well prepared to tackle the problems and enemies before them in the 'Promised Land'. Those years were to be shared with their children, for they grew to become millions of hardened, desert nomads with all the skills of nomadic life, to be inherited eventually by the Bedouins. I will not recount all their adventures over these years, faithfully and patiently guided by Moses, who had to sacrifice himself in his devotion to Yahweh's task. The high spot was the scene at Mount Sinai, when Yahweh called to Moses to ascend the mountain to meet him personally, to receive Yahweh's commandments inscribed by Him on two stone tablets. Only to find on his long-awaited descent, that those errant Children of Israel had reverted to the worship of 'graven images'. They had forced Aaron to melt down all their gold ornaments, and cast them in the shape of a golden calf, around which they danced, wined and celebrated in the most sinful fashion.

When he glimpsed this hellish sight, Moses' patience snapped and he hurled the tablets to the ground. At this point and in such temper, he was ready to punish severely. For the first time he called on his Levites to kill neighbour, brother to kill brother, until 3000 had been slain. He smashed the calf image, ground it to dust and mixed it with water, which every calf worshipper had to drink. But when Yahweh demanded yet again, 'Off with their heads', Moses once more pleaded for his wayward people, to avoid their total destruction at the hands of Yahweh. Even though he was himself offered a new rôle, to produce a new nation of his own, a temptation difficult to resist – to generate your own new world which might include your own immortality. But wise Moses was already witness to the destructive hot temper of Yahweh, and the invalidity of his covenants and promises, to envisage Yahweh's threatened wholesale massacre of his entire people.

The final blow for both Moses and his multitude, who must by now have swollen to more than 2 million, came in Moab before the Promised Land. Moses sent out spies to check the land, peoples and food conditions. Returning, they reported it a land 'flowing with milk and honey', but peopled by giants, constantly fighting each other. All told gloomy, fearful stories except Joshua and Caleb, who were optimistic of success. But they were the minority. The Israelites chose to believe the others' grim tales of giant, fierce warriors ready to kill them; became fearful and hysterical, and demanded to return to Egypt under a new leader. However, they did not deserve the mass slaughter carried out by Yahweh, thus breaking his greatest, repeated promise to them over their 40 years of homeless wandering in that desolate wasteland.

Yahweh, fully enraged, now condemned them all to die in the Wilderness, except Joshua and Caleb. Only their children would now be allowed to enter the Promised Land. So, once more, Yahweh's covenant with the Children of Israel, and all his promises, went for naught. After slavery followed by all those long, weary, hungry years in the Wilderness, they now learn that it was all in vain. What sort of saviour from Egyptian bondage was this, to be left to die in the Wilderness in sight of the Promised Land? As for Moses, his 'reward' was to be just the sight of the Promised Land from a hilltop, then quick death, to be buried by Yahweh in an unmarked, secret grave. But J gives our hero Moses the last word. Moses is so moved by his forced removal from his people, on whom he has lavished all his care over 40 long, difficult years, that he insists on making his unforgettable and most moving farewell speech. Later writers deemed this of such great, outstanding importance for the future of his people, that Exodus was extended to include all details of his final blessing and exhortation in Deuteronomy. Thus ended J's everlasting contribution to our Bible.

2

THE AUTHORS OF THE PENTATEUCH

No Hebrew literature has ever been discovered before the time of David. J was the first-known author of the opening books of the Bible, including Genesis, Exodus and Numbers, of which Leviticus and Deuteronomy are extensions. He produced his original manuscript about 920 BC at the Court of Solomon's son Rehoboam in Jerusalem. However, large libraries of earlier clay tablets in cuneiform script have been unearthed in recent years, especially in royal palaces at Nineveh, Ashur and Babylon. They tell of almost identical ancient myths and folklore to that of the Creation. The largest, the *Epic of Gilgamesh*, was found in Nineveh palace library in 1872 by George Smith.

This relates the story of Gilgamesh, semi-divine King of Uruk, at about 2800 BC. His great friend Enkidu's death causes him to go in search of immortality. He finds Utnapishtim, sole survivor of a great flood, sent by the gods to punish mankind. The god Ea warns Utnapishtim of the approaching catastrophe, and instructs him to build a boat (giving exact dimensions), leave his possessions and select living things to save. When the flood comes, his boat floats for six days and seven nights. Then he sends forth a raven, then a dove, which does not return. Noah does likewise. It survives to prove the ordeal over. This story is amazingly close to Noah and the Flood, and must have been known to J, and was clearly used by him.

43

The *Epic of Creation* tells of the beginning of the world and the building of the great city of Babylon, under the protection of Marduk, king of the gods. Marduk says: 'Let me put blood together and make bones too. Let me set up primeval man; man shall be his name.' Thus man is created to do the hard work of the gods, so that they may now be at leisure. Similar concept and a close relationship to J's Creation. Surely Yahweh owes much to Marduk, king of the gods.

Much of the *Epic of Creation* is concerned with religious matters. Gods played a major part in the life of the ancient world. This Epic is more advanced in perception. Its Beginning bears close relationship to J.

'When skies above were not yet named
Nor Earth below pronounced by name'

George Smith discovered the library of tablets containing the story of the Flood, fitting into the Gilgamesh Epic. Also the Chaldean story of the Creation, telling of man's original innocence when created from clay by their god and filled with the breath of life. Followed by their story of the temptation and the fall. The Sumerians seem to have been the first and ultimate leaders in their invention of much of our heritage. We owe a tremendous debt to those little black-haired people who invaded Mesopotamia (possibly from the Indus valley), about 5000 BC. They proved to be the most innovative of our earliest ancestors, highly imaginative and gifted, producing the first known form of writing in cuneiform script of over 100 characters, in which they became extremely proficient in daily use.

The *Epic of Creation* bears striking similarity to the creation of man in Genesis as portrayed by J. Professor Dr F. Delitsch maintained in his lecture 'Babel or Bible' (1902), that the Bible was proven to be not the oldest book, but was preceded by literature from a much earlier epoch. There were great similarities, but the Old Testament could no longer be regarded as unique. For the first time the authenticity of the Bible was questioned. J's source material was now revealed, throwing fresh doubts on the originality of all his 'Beginning' of Creation of the world and mankind.

Theodor Gaster in his book *Myth, Legend and Custom in the Old Testament*, quotes the reading of the Septuagint and some other Ancient Versions, as also a Hebrew fragment discovered at Qumran (Biblica 36) as follows: Moses farewell song, Deuteronomy 32:7-14, chides the Israelites for their ingratitude and infidelity to Yahweh and sings:

'When the Most High Elyôn doled out the nations,
parcelled out the human race,
He fixed the bounds of peoples by the number of the gods.
Then (this) people of his became Yahweh's share Jacob his
allotted estate.'

Thus 'The Most High God Elyôn' (pre-Israelites) was regarded as the Supreme God, with Yahweh as subordinate member of the pantheon.

Later Hebrew text reads: 'By the number of the Children of Israel.'

This surely bears out the case, previously stated, for a Supreme Spirit overall. Again, in Genesis 14:1, Melchizedek, King of Salem, is clearly described as: 'priest of God Most High. And he blessed him and said: Blessed be Abram of God Most High, possessor of heaven and earth.'

There appears a significant difference between the God Most

45

High and Yahweh, commonly called the Lord in the later version.

Psalm 82:6: the supernal gods are styled 'Sons of Elyôn'. In the Talmud, it is the appellation of angels.

By comparison, in the Babylonian *Epic of Creation* it parallels the notion that the earth was parcelled out among the gods when Marduk (their principal god) divided the 600 gods under him into equal celestial and terrestrial companies, allotting them their several portions.

This points to my earlier assumption that J envisaged and inherited the notion of a Supreme Spirit, invisible and unseen, directing the movements of the whole universe and the galaxies and controlling all the planets. So that Yahweh was given his own separate mission of Creation of our world and all therein – with similarity to the older legends like Marduk's apportionment.

Darwin's *The Origin of Species* proved that the Earth was millions of years old, against all previous belief. His factual evidence also undermined the myth of the Creation. Life must have evolved gradually over a long period. Such scientific discovery and factual presentation caused people to begin to question the hitherto accepted belief in the Bible and its credibility. There was no longer a general acceptance. The ancient belief that the world and mankind were formed by an instantaneous stroke of magic no longer held good. Mythology has little defence against scientific fact.

The Flood story is matched also in other myths such as the Akkadian Atrahasis ('Extra Wise'), and the Sumerian Ziusudra ('Long Life'). Atrahasis is a similar, Noah-like figure of outstanding significance. In fact, many Flood stories have been clearly revealed as J's source of material for his own version. The Sumerian story of 'Enki and Ninhursag', a Paradise in the land of Dilmun (reportedly Bahrain), bears close resemblance to J's Garden of Eden. Early Bronze Age settlements of about 2500 BC have been found in this area. There is also evidence that the last glaciers melted about 10,000 BC and flooded the Earth. It has even been suggested that American Indians owed their origin to some of the lost tribes of Israel in exile. They had their own epics of floods from the melting of American glaciers. The Nile flooded regularly every year until the building, eventually, of the Aswan Dam. Likewise the Tigris and Euphrates, affecting the whole area including Iraq, and the Chaldees.

It is obvious that J owed much to those very intelligent, advanced Sumerians, who not only invented the art of writing but also the wheel, first coinage and the plough, and had mathematical knowledge and great engineering ability. They had their own special gods but no supreme deity. Had they been left in peace to pursue their own advancement, our world might well have developed differently, with their continuous progress to the general good. But their very success provoked envy and greed from others, who could not rest content until Ur, their capital, had been sacked, burnt and ruined. Fortunately their clay tablets did not suffer unduly, becoming baked hard in the heat, and were thus preserved to tell us about this civilised people, and record their enterprises and achievements. Where, then, are the tablets of the early Hebrews? Were they all mercilessly destroyed by their enemies?

J now emerges as an anonymous author, simply called J because he belonged to the tribe of Judah. He was the first and greatest Hebrew author, with a talent of genius, who fashioned the framework of the unique history and religion of Judaism. Although altered, amended and even drastically changed in parts by later writers, his basic original authorship of the greatest epic of the birth, growth and development of the Hebrew faith, remains largely unchallenged. Especially after what I call his mythical Prologue, from the Beginning of Genesis up to and including Noah and the Flood, and his entertaining additional tale of the pyramidal ziggurat of Babel, similar to those recorded earlier in Ur and Babylon.

As we have seen, J owed much of his first inspiration to his knowledge and study of the stories of Creation and Flood, so well recorded by other countries, as quoted above. Nevertheless, he shows remarkable insight into human nature, and paints with unerring accuracy his many portraits of individuals and characters, immediately recognisable still in our own era. Their characteristics, strengths and weaknesses, are repeated through all ages, including their leaders, whether of countries, communities, religions or industry. We warm to J's characters, emerging from ancient history, because we see ourselves clearly reflected and mirrored in them. Clone Yahwehs are matched in different religions, still behaving in similar fashion, from fanatics preaching violence, to the patient, wise, leadership of good, forbearing and tolerantly forgiving deities.

J's leaders vary from strong and weak kings, petty dictators gaining power by force, bribery and corruption ('every man has his price'), to extremists of one fanatical persuasion or other. Thence to the scarce quota of wise heads, who guide their charges patiently and intelligently, like Moses, along the right paths. J is a true democrat, often producing his best leaders, such as David and Ezra (priest, scribe and prophet), both originally simple shepherds, straight from the ranks of ordinary people.

No wonder Shakespeare sought and found many of his best characters within the stories of the Geneva Bible of 1560 after

Miles Coverdale, and the scholarly rendering of the Pentateuch by William Tyndall in 1530. They bear close relationship
to those early biblical men and women, kings and warriors, in
all their human behaviour. They all move in sequence through
the pages of the Bible, still universally acknowledged as the
greatest book ever written, led by J's original men and
women, plucked from our ancient ancestors, into the pages of
our modern history (*'plus ça change'*), and far superior to any
of those mythical creatures from whom J obviously found
some of his sources. He used, but rose above them in his
superior creation. But we do not yet know all his source
material, especially concerning Yahweh, who is obviously
closely related to the earlier manlike, aggressive, demanding,
arbitrary gods.

Myths and folklore are linked in J's panorama to real history.
He criticises fearlessly Yahweh and all humans alike, from
cunning Jacob (such a complex being) to the quarrelling sons
of Solomon who split asunder David's great kingdom, fast
becoming an empire, driven by jealousy and greed, and
leading inevitably to the final downfall and exile. From the
all-conquering, doughty, victorious fighters marshalled under
Joshua to win their Promised Land (it surely needed the moral
and physical strength trained into the sons and heirs of those
erstwhile slaves of Egyptian bondage, to withstand the continuous attacks of the fierce tribes they encountered as they
battled their way through the bitter opposition of Canaan and
into Palestine), to the mighty victories of King David, down
to the final sacking of Jerusalem and destruction of the
Temple in 70 AD, to the conclusive Exile of 135 AD and the
Diaspora, by decree of the Emperor Hadrian, after the final
revolt of Bar Kochba.

Condemned to wander the world in a new Wilderness, seeking
shelter wherever possible – only to be spurned, harried,

tortured, assassinated everywhere; from Spain's torturing Inquisition and ill-treatment throughout Europe, to the final, brutal, total mass-murder of 6 million innocent men, women, even babes in arms, in that vilest of all, Nazi German Holocaust – a devilish deed now stamped indelibly on the German and world conscience. They finally found lasting shelter, first in America, the only country to offer them real succour and welcome, then, less open-handedly but still helpful, in Britain and more grudgingly elsewhere, and finally back home at last in Israel.

There has never been such a world story, moving from the Beginning to what we now hope to be the final peaceful settlement, back in their eternal 'Promised Land' of Israel, at peace with all their neighbours, especially the Arabs, who owe similar descent from Abraham ('Father of All Nations') and are thus their Semitic blood brothers, descended from the same father, producing both Isaac and Ishmael.

Yet, through all those hard years of suffering, torture, Inquisition, pogroms and final mass-murders, J's first Hebrews, descended from Abraham, throughout their tragic yet heroic history, have held steadfast to their religion, faith, laws and customs. To these they have clung tenaciously, through all hardships, from their original 'Jacob become Israel' after his mighty, night-long struggle with Yahweh's messenger at Penuel, to their final return now to their ancient homeland of Israel, their 'Promised Land'.

J portrays the amazingly quick development of his people in a single generation, from a small tribal grouping into an international power of remarkable expansion, only finally reduced by the failure of David's successors to live up to his great eminence. He lived some 450 years before the Redactor, who produced his final composite form of the Pentateuch, with the first actual Bible. Still accepted as the basic instrument of worship in the greatest part of our world, despite the number of different versions split off from the first, ancient and original form.

J originally began by gathering together the myths and folklore of the legendary background to his Creation. Above all, his Yahweh rises above all others of those early gods who were manlike in appearance and emotions. Yet he still seems to inherit from them many of his expressions, dynamic orders, actions and reactions, violent outbursts of temper (like Bull-el) and harsh punishments, meted out regardless of status, for major and minor offences, by the erring behaviour of his creatures. J's stories were captivating epics of the Creation, Patriarchs, Joseph and Moses *inter alia*, unadorned but often poetic styling. Unlike his successors, who were all priestly scribes, he was not a religious writer. He established his historical/religious framework for others to follow, in so telling a fashion and style that none could deny him his authorship, though they all sought to change, add, amend or alter to suit their own priestly self-interest. Basically they all had to accept J's original work as genuinely authentic. J stands out therefore as unique and original, in true eminence as the first and greatest Jewish author.

Much effort was obviously needed to rework the oral traditions of the distant past. From these, with the aid of his neighbours' similar stories, he developed his own Creation (culled in different format from other versions), which has been almost universally accepted by the following generations of Jews, Christians and Muslims alike. Yet there is no personal record of himself. We can only seek to gauge his character and personality from his actual writings, of which, fortunately, much has been discovered. This marks him out as of high standing, intelligence and unique inventive ability.

Little is known of Rehoboam and his Court, and indeed of all the Royal Courts, except that of Solomon. No scribe has left us detailed descriptions or diaries like Pepys, unlike later world writers, who seem to delight in fulsome descriptions of the daily life and gossip of royal courts. The tenure of those ancient Jewish courts was usually so short and insecure, with continual battles for existence, and much time spent in defence against everlasting threats and imminence of attack on all sides. So there was little chance of a settled existence after David and Solomon, who remain their greatest, and longest-lasting kings and leaders.

J does not usurp Yahweh's rôle in condemning the malefactors, be they king, priest or people. His characters are delineated in all their strengths, weaknesses and idiosyncrasies, good and evil deeds, general behaviour and reaction to Yahweh, relieved by dexterous lightness of touch and description, with his ironic humour underlying all his work. He spares none, but as a true historian, offers no personal criticism – not even of his hero David's unworthy conduct in his affair with Bathsheba and murderous removal of Uriah, her soldier husband. But he ensures that Yahweh's punishment is duly meted out and David humbled and severely punished by Yahweh, even to the death of his sons, a drastic stroke.

He portrays the tragic as well as the comic, which he obviously enjoys in his uproarious tale of Balaam's talking ass, or Sarai's admonishment of Yahweh for promising husband Abraham a son for her, despite her barrenness of 90 years (with Abraham then 100). He depicts the remarkable contrast and irony of this courageous Abraham daring to bargain with Yahweh before the proposed destruction of Sodom and Gomorrah. What a revelation in creativity is his scenario where crafty uncle Laban forces Jacob to work for him seven years for his beloved Rachel, then tricks him into marrying the veiled Leah, before demanding a further stint of seven years for Rachel – who then seeks her own revenge on her cheating father. Or his unearthly story of Jacob, the heel-clutcher and a wily trickster from birth, and his transformation into goodly Israel (God-clutcher), after his night-long 'testing' struggle with the stranger (Yahweh's angel), sent to try him at Penu-el. Suddenly his hitherto minor rôle became that of the major creation of the future Israel. Truly a masterly composition.

J is the unique, outstanding, original author, above all others in the Bible. There is none like him, none to match him, and he rightfully takes his place among the world's greatest writers, but with no thought of becoming world-famous. Above all, he abhors violence, which is never allowed to go unpunished. But, unlike those later great world authors, whose work continued unchanged and unchallenged, growing in fame and reputation, J's work was altered, part-eliminated and gradually reduced in substance and recognition, over the following generations of priestly interference and power drive. Finally to be carved up by the rabbis of the 2nd century AD, who ensured an almost complete change from J's original Yahweh to their more acceptable priestly version of the distant, unseen Adonai, now almost unrecognisable from J's monotheistic 'down to earth' deity.

J was an objective historian, coolly assessing his subjects, with no personal aims or power objective of his own. He was the sole, original lay author. He tended to paint his pictures in clear strokes of black and white. Many of these portrayals of people of his era strike a familiar note in all ages following, right through to the present. P, the priestly writers, were subjective, seeking their own desired form for Yahweh – to be detached from human contact, to act and be heard entirely through the priesthood. They sought to act as his deputies.

But then began a separate, internecine contest and power struggle between the two rival priestly camps: the Mushite followers of Moses against the Aaronite followers of Aaron (all Levites), each declaring to be the rightful possessors of priestly power, with the right to influence kings and leaders as well as the people, as lawful representatives of Yahweh.

E, the Elohist, who wrote about 850 BC, was a descendant of Moses, and a Mushite priest. He accepted J's version almost wholly, so that henceforth their versions became regarded jointly as J/E. As opposed to all other priestly versions, which all came from Aaronite priests under P. Jeremiah, the great prophet, along with most others, regarded these Aaronite priests with contempt for tampering with the original version by J, and admonished them for altering its truth to suit their own ends. E came down from Shiloh, main centre for all Mushite priests led by Abiathar, David's High Priest (deposed by Solomon for supporting his brother Adonijah for David's throne). Named E because he first used the plural Elohim for God, until later switching to J's Yahweh. He rarely differed from J, except for insisting that in the Creation, man came first; followed by plants, vegetation and animals, and finally by woman, created from Adam, to be his companion in Eden. E also wrote the amusing tale of the sons of Elohim lusting after the young maidens on earth. This resulted in a number of odd-shaped giants who soon perished. The later tales of similar exploits by the Greek gods bore great similarity.

P, the priests' representative of the Aaronites, followed much later, c 550 BC. P reshaped J and E's Beginning to suit his own priestly concept. He concentrated in his Creation story more on water, air, the heavens and the seas, as of primary conception. His priestly group were responsible, apparently, for writing the Book of Leviticus as their special vehicle, detailing the extent and circumstance to be assumed of priestly

54

power, duties, responsibilities, and especially their rights and dues from the people. They carefully carved out for themselves and their heirs and successors through history, a safe, snug profession fully protected and cared for by the people at all times henceforth. It was then confined to the tribe of Levi, but such a comfortable, protected profession was quickly noted and copied elsewhere, spreading quickly around the world. It did not take long before Jeremiah and other prophets (who cared naught for money or possessions or protection, but passionately for their religious beliefs) began to upbraid the sinful priests, who sought primarily to secure for themselves a life of luxury, fully fed, clothed and supported in every way by the people.

D, the supposed author of Deuteronomy, about 650 BC, devoted most of his Book to the last days of Moses, as an extension of J's Exodus. It is obvious that J covered it all in his manuscript, so it is somewhat puzzling as to how and why (and when) J's total work, unbroken in its sequence, was divided from J's complete, continuous Epic into five separate books. D was specially interested in consideration of various aspects of war and combat. He detailed the Laws of War with special concession to be granted to any man who feared war and physical combat. He was to be excused, and exempted from conscription and military service, on the grounds that his fear would affect his comrades, who might be intimidated and lose their courage and zest for battle. It is strange how quickly such fear is felt, and tends either to spread, or to cause violent reaction in contempt of 'cowards'. D maintained that it was far better for such men to be usefully employed where they might best serve the community, and leave the fighting to those able and willing and best equipped to fight in support of their cause. Such wisdom was later lost, unfortunately, and this wise law revoked. As a result many men have since been put to death as cowards, from complete misunderstanding of their true mental state and feelings, when their abilities might have been put to better use and value to the community. Some of the 'pacifist' stretcher bearers in World War II were amongst the truly brave, risking their lives under fire to rescue the wounded.

D also dealt with and clarified certain other problems of war, such as how to differentiate between and control units of armed forces. An especial problem arises from those who seek to punish, kill or wound their defeated enemy, and those prepared to spare and possibly forgive erstwhile foes, after time for proper, cool judgement has been allowed. Such judgement is often extremely difficult to observe sensibly, in the height of the violence of battle. D's version of his deity was confused between justice and divine mercy (of which little had so far been shown), leading to some bewildering conflicts between divine and human relationships.

The Jews have so often been placed in such severe situations whereby, as innocent victims, they have been forced to endure insults, wounding and plain, unadulterated murder throughout history. How often they have forgiven their enemies and returned good for evil, only to suffer further recurrence of brutality, torture or even mass extermination. Yet they still survive, and the world slowly begins to recognise its fault, stemming from the religious persecution begun by the Church, established by Stephen and Paul. Only now, at the end of 20 centuries, is the true extent of the horrible crimes against the innocents becoming clearly known and understood. At last, true contrite spirit is being shown by the Church for its crimes, so that we may hope that all may be forgiven by the Jewish people who have suffered enough since their final forced exile from their Promised Land. At least they must now be allowed to live in peace, in their return to their full (though so small) portion of their original Israel, with the co-

56

operation and amity of their neighbours. The whole of Israel is less than the size of Wales.

Yahweh is represented by J as anthropomorphic, semi-human, walking and talking in person with Adam and Eve, with Abram, wrestling with Jacob at Penu-el and renaming him Israel – even allowing Esau to bargain away his blessing rights for a mess of pottage (hardly believable, no matter how good a salesman Jacob may then have been). Or was J seeking to present us with a hidden meaning within these early puzzles? There is an obvious affinity between J's version and that of the corresponding stories of the Creation by others such as the Sumerians, Akkadians, Assyrians and Persians, especially the *Epic of Gilgamesh*. So J must have drawn inspiration from all these similar stories and epics, including especially the Flood, and Noah's counterpart, Utnapishtim.

The Redactor, who lived about 400 BC and produced the finally accepted, composite rendition of the Pentateuch, was thought to be Ezra, the Aaronite priest, prophet and scribe. He extracted what he considered to be the best accounts of all the writers, and combined them into his final version. Much of the original J version was thereby lost, but even after more than 500 years, the Redactor could not depart very far (except principally the handling of the Yahweh situation), from J's text.

The Redactor finally combined the work of all the previous writers from J to E, D and P. He thought it wiser to detach the end of J's Moses from Exodus, because he felt it of great importance to give more space to extend full value of J's farewell passages from the great leader. Also his final details of instructions to his people on their future conduct and behaviour, following all Yahweh's Law and Commandments (which seem to be more negative 'Thou shalt nots' than the positive code of conduct laid down by Moses, their great leader), and keeping their religious laws and customs, with daily observance.

This final version continued to be accepted to the end of the first millennium. It was only when the famous group of learned rabbis came together in the second century AD, that a very different version appeared. These rabbis could not accept J's version of Yahweh, and they altered, changed and then eliminated him completely but too drastically. Yet in their final version they still had to leave the main text of J, with his ring of authenticity, eloquent characterisations, unsurpassable stories and portrayals, almost as he wrote them. They tried to modify some of the strange stories, such as the lustful Elohim's sons chasing the earthly maidens and producing unearthly giants; and the crafty, deceitful Patriarchs and some of his ambitious women (in whom J seemed particularly to delight). But they could not accept his murderous founders of the tribes of Israel, nor yet a drunken Noah, or worse still a raging, bloodthirsty Yahweh, sometimes quite out of control. This raw version would never do for their concept of a Bible fit to present to all their people. J, of course, did not believe in concealing good or bad points and imperfections. But he was long gone, and the new breed of priests were not prepared to leave it to the people themselves to judge and decide. How like our present world situation, with governments and rulers quite unable and unprepared to let the people have a say in final decisions.

J reveals a revulsion against violence. He does not believe that his Yahweh owns us, as Balaam owns his ass. We humans have free will, a mind to think, a mouth to speak and the ability to decide for ourselves. He obviously disapproves of the severe punishment meted out by Yahweh for minor offences, without consideration or tolerance, such as that of

Baal-peor. He later compares that incident of transgression with the situation at the same area, where Yahweh finally and secretly buries his most faithful servant, the greatest leader Moses, degraded to death in this unhallowed spot (whilst still strong and alert), unknown, even to his family, against all Jewish custom, in an unmarked grave. Moses is allowed sight of the Promised Land, but forced to hand over to Joshua, his lieutenant, after all those lonely 40 years of leadership, ever-suffering under the lash of an impatient, intolerant Yahweh, who obviously bears him grudges for his refusal to accept and obey Yahweh's constantly reiterated orders to hang, decapitate or kill off his own creation, the Children of Israel.

J had no real heroes except David, and to a lesser degree, Moses. But he had many heroines. Sarai, Isaac's Rebecca (famous for the scene at the well at Haran), Jacob's Rachel, for love of whom, this self-seeking cheater of Esau was willing to work for the cunning Laban not seven but fourteen years. She repaid him by stealing her father's most precious possession, his household 'graven' gods. Courageous Zipporah, who saved her husband Moses from the two would-be assassins sent by Yahweh, with the bloody circumcision scene! Ruth, the Moabite married to Boaz and, with her intermarriage, becoming ancestress to David. Tamar, married into Judah's family, loses Er and then his brother Oman. Having no husband and still no child, she plans to trap her father-in-law, now a widower, into marriage. What a clever plot J unfolds, as Tamar, fully veiled as a Canaanite prostitute, tempts Judah on his way to sheep-shearing. Afterwards she is able to prove her case, with the production of his stick and seal, that he left behind as a pledge. She now bears Pharez in the direct line of succession to David – who seems to be the outstanding product of mixed marriages. Also brave Esther, who wins the heart of King Ahasuerus and, as his wife, is able to foil the dastardly plot of Haman to kill all the

Jews in Persia – to be repeated in modern Iran and Iraq. These madmen produce clones from Haman to Hitler. The heroines are all dynamic characters, bolstering up their husbands, and driving them and themselves on to success. J's heroines each deserves the place and position she fights to win, usually outwitting the men concerned, as later did Deborah, the warlike judge.

Abram, however, was no hero. He was plainly a family man of real courage, leading a well-ordered and contented existence, and surprised to be given the honour of a call from Yahweh. His strength lies in the fact that he is the first to recognise and accept the monotheistic deity, and prepared to follow whatever instructions he may receive. He does not argue about leaving Ur of the Chaldees, with his father Terah and family, to settle in Haran. Then to leave the safety and comfort of his home and move, as directed, towards Canaan, which is to become the Promised Land for his descendants.

It is astonishing that Yahweh, as sign of his promise to Abraham of his great future for his descendants, did not arrange the earlier birth of at least one male child to poor Sarai, suffering under the burden of her barrenness, regarding herself as unfulfilled, and failing her husband in not providing him with a male successor. Yet, despite his promise, Yahweh makes her wait until 90 before 'arranging' a birth. Abram was already 75 when he received Yahweh's call to leave Haran and move towards Canaan. Sarai must have been over 65 when they went to Egypt because of the famine. So it seems a somewhat imaginative story of Abram calling her his sister, because he was afraid of the misconduct of the Egyptians. How could one accept that Pharaoh, entranced by her beauty, decided to take her into his household – only to be visited with a plague by Yahweh. Unless their time measure differed radically from ours.

What emerges is the obvious cunning manoeuvre by Abram:
'And Abram was very rich in cattle, in silver, and in gold.'
(Genesis 13:3) So expanded is he that must now separate his
possessions from nephew Lot, who chooses the rich Jordan
area, known as Sodom, unaware of the evil nature of its
inhabitants.

Now we embark on the unexpected interpolation, without any
specific reason, of the bloodthirsty battles between nine kings.
The defeated regather strength and allies for further battles,
including the kings of Sodom and Gomorrah. Defeated, they
flee, only to fall into lime pits: 'And others took Lot.... and
his goods, and departed.' (Genesis 14) J now shows us the
courageous Abram who, with 318 trained men, pursued the
enemy to Dan 'and smote them'. 'And he brought back all the
goods, and also brought back his brother Lot and his goods,
and the women also, and the people.' (Genesis 14:16) Note the
goods were of first importance, then Lot and finally 'the
women also', as an afterthought. More of J's ironic humour.
Clearly Abram had by then a considerable entourage to be
able to muster an immediate assault force of 318 trained,
armed men.

Abram has also the courage to grumble at fierce Yahweh
directly that he has not been given an heir to all his possessions, despite all Yahweh's promises for his 'descendants'. But
Yahweh has not yet finished with imposing further burdens on
his long-suffering servant. After finally giving old Sarai her
long-desired only son, at the incredible age of 90, Yahweh
later demands the final sacrifice of Isaac, their beloved son
and heir. Abraham is now ordered to build an altar, bind
Isaac, and then kill him as human sacrifice to his God. Isaac,
now a grown man, questions his loving father about the
missing sacrifice, but seems not to object nor complain at
learning his own fate.

To our utter amazement, Abraham appears to comply without demur. How could he possibly face such a devastating murder of his only son (by the way, now about 30), and then go home to face Sarah, his wife? It is impossible to believe, even though Yahweh breaks the final tension, by changing the sacrifice to the ram, suddenly caught by its horns in a nearby bush. One is tempted to say: 'Now, J, you are surely stretching it too far this time. We know your Yahweh seems to delight in testing his servants to ensure they have the courage and bravery to carry out his ever-demanding missions – but really, to expect us to believe that father Abraham would consent, without even putting up an argument, to the murder of his sole beloved son – is quite beyond our acceptance.' Another of Yahweh's incomprehensible tests, but maybe wise old Abraham could now read him better, and play the same game with assured judgement that Yahweh would not kill off the instrument of his future plans.

No wonder Abraham now hastens to get Isaac married and productive of children, before Yahweh can impose any more burdens. This may have strengthened Abraham's attitude, for, when we next encounter him, he is really putting up an argument with Yahweh against his proposed total destruction of Sodom and Gomorrah. J was quite concerned with family relations, unlike P, a major successor, who sought priestly power as an Aaronite, and was more motivated by seeking a rôle as deputy to Yahweh, to demand disciplined obedience of the people to the Laws, with the priests acting, as it were, *in loco parentis*.

J's story from Creation to Exodus covers the principal characters from Abraham, chosen 'Father of All Nations', to Moses, leading the Children of Israel out of bondage to their Promised Land, after 40 years' hard training. J's Yahweh bears little resemblance to the god of Ezra, later priestly scribe

62

and prophet (and possibly also the Redactor), who set the shape of the final edition with his Bible, which was generally accepted as the authentic version until the turn of the first century.

The later Rabbis would not accept J's original stories of talking animals, the lustful Elohim of E, nor the deceitful Patriarchs, all J's ambitious women, the murderous founders of the tribes of Israel, a drunken Noah, a raging, hot-tempered, punishing Yahweh, sometimes out of control, or the many false witnesses and self-seekers. J would never hide any imperfections – unlike P, who, as an Aaronite priest, could not accept them, and would not allow the people and lay writers to judge, and so wrote his own version to suit his Aaronite group. The rabbis set out to define the Laws and customs more exactly and to 'put a fence around the Law', to keep the Jewish people inside, and guard against break-ins from the outside world. At the same time, to prevent their people wandering forth and seeking other gods.

J emerges from the Bible as the true originator, designer and architect of the Jewish religion, beyond his mythical tales and ancient folklore. His pieces fit the complicated puzzle of those problematic first years of birth and development, with all those boring 'begats', to portray the gradual gathering together of this unique people from Abram to Moses. Then to the final disaster of the Exile, condemning the 'Chosen People' to wander the face of the Earth in suffering, torture and murder, until their return at long last, to their God-given home of Israel. The fragments of J's writings, so aptly portrayed by Professors H. Bloom and D. Rosenberg in their scholarly book, illustrate the many-faceted character, whom I regard as more important than most of those he described so graphically. Their well-researched *Book of J* reveals them both as really ironic figures in the unequivocally

63

Jewish tradition. Their scholarly skill and insight are truly outstanding.

J was fortunate in living and writing in that wondrous city of Jerusalem, with all its magic, inspired by David. It still acts as a magnet to the world, drawing all to this centre of the world's first and foremost monotheistic faith and people. There lived the 'People of the Bible', witnessing and developing in those great events and the gradual unfolding of their history, before the Western world had begun. If only our archaeologists could transport us back to the real ancient Israel, to see and witness the truth, beginning with those ancient Hibarus, it would surely reveal the true, exciting story of the Creation and all that happened 'In the Beginning'. They have already unearthed so much, but still need a greater effort to produce at least the ancient tablet equivalent of the Dead Sea Scrolls – which still remain a mystery, as yet only partly revealed.

The genius of J as a storyteller was his skill in combining dramatic scenes of creation, heroic deeds, tragedy and transgression, wars, and eternal conflict with romance, sacrifice, personal ambition, all shades of human nature and, above all, with a light touch of humour. His grim story of Yahweh's destruction of almost all his Creation by pouring down rain to cause death by drowning (a method he is to use again) in the great Flood, makes one gasp with horror at such coldly planned violence. It is lightened slightly at the end by Noah's celebratory drunken orgy, on release from his pent-up prison in the Ark for 40 days and nights. (The numbers 40, 7 and 12 are repeated often in the Bible.)

Then the ironic, somewhat grisly, humour of Abraham daring to bargain, for the first and only time, with Yahweh, for the lives of the sinful people as they walk the road to Sodom.

Even this awesome story has its counterpart elsewhere, turning to salt or stone those who disobey prescribed orders of deities, as with Lot's inquisitive wife.

These, like the amusing story of Balaam's talking ass, are examples of J's deft touches of genius, unmatched anywhere in the Bible. Who else could equal the renowned story of Solomon's wise judgement in the case of the two women equally claiming the child? In such gleaming colours is painted Solomon's great kingdom, palaces, riches, jewels and gold ornaments, and his great Temple of Yahweh, built in the years of his growing greatness – only to presage the darker shades of Solomon's fall from grace to greed and luxury, sexual extravagance, with supposedly 700 concubines and 300 wives. Brutal taxation and forced labour of his subjects followed his mounting debts, to the imposed sale of parts of his kingdom to his friend Hiram, the king of Tyre. But, worst of all, he falls to the worship of his wives' false gods, which spells the end of him and his erstwhile blessing from Yahweh.

The tragic result is the splitting of his kingdom by his sons, who divide it into Israel and Judah, with foregone conclusion of the fate of a house divided. J must have sat in the court of King Rehoboam in Jerusalem, mourning the loss of northern Israel, with its ten tribes who seem to have vanished without trace. He was witnessing the gradual disintegration of his hero David's great Empire. No wonder he spent much time researching the past, to shut out the unhappy present. He thus found his true métier in his writing. Doubtless he was a scribe at court, but with no priestly affinity. So he was free to seek out the truth of the past, such as he could discover from oral tradition, and the first written records of the Sumerians and their neighbours. He filled gaps with his own experiences and imaginative creativeness, thus producing the all-time masterpiece of this tenth century genius.

The pity is that only fragmented pieces have been discovered, though sufficient to arrive at the greater part of his work, which has to remain anonymous until more scrolls are found to fill in those gaps, and reveal his identity and details of his life and times. There may well be some underlying meaning to his work. Certainly his complex character Yahweh warrants much closer study. We must remember that he doubtless wrote for his own personal satisfaction, as well as for those of his own generation, sufficiently educated to read and comprehend his work and thoughts. There was certainly no apparent criticism of his book for hundreds of years, until the Aaronite priests produced their very personal versions of Creation. Nor could he foresee that, like Shakespeare, Homer, Dante, Molière, Goethe, all such world-famous, prolifically read authors (who all, similarly, only wrote for their own generations), his work would live on to be discovered and read, with wonder and admiration, hundreds of years later, despite many priestly efforts to erase them.

Exodus dates 480 years before the foundation of the Temple, in the fourth year of Solomon's reign. Jericho, the oldest city, fell 400 years before Solomon to Joshua, who fought his way through Canaan to the Promised Land of Palestine, their final goal, to become the Land of Israel, given by God. What a fantastic epic story is the Exodus, which has caught the imagination of the whole world. Still repeated every year by Jewish families everywhere, as well as other faiths, who also celebrate the seven days of Passover. What an epic struggle between Pharaoh and Moses (speaking for Yahweh), 'Let my people go', to the final tragedy of that Passover night, to succeed at last in breaking Pharaoh's stubborn will. Despite the powers of J's astounding imagination, there is no disguising the basic facts of this, one of the strangest, most extraordinary accounts of the Bible. No other similar or matching stories have ever been found, to discount or weaken J's most powerful epic.

What we, of course, know, is that those poor released prisoners must now face 40 hard, long, relentless years of suffering in the desolate Wilderness, until some begin to wonder whether it was all worthwhile. Only once again to face the wrath and punishment of Yahweh. Who can but feel the pain, sorrow and anguish of those hard years of painful survival, growing old, tired and pessimistic of ever reaching this reiterated promise of the land flowing with milk and honey? We are not told how many perished on the way, despite the endless stream of 'begats' in Numbers.

Forty long weary years and then, at the end, neither they nor their patient, long-suffering, great leader, Moses, will be permitted to enter the Promised Land. Again we ask: what sort of Yahweh was this, to boast of freeing them from slavery and then to make them suffer the hardships, hunger, thirst and misery of that desolate Wilderness, only to be refused entry to the Promised Land after 40 long, wearisome years? What poor compensation that their children may now enter, but without them, who have suffered and sacrificed in vain. It was as though the gates of Paradise (or Heaven), were being shut in their faces. It really does not bear consideration of any possible reason. Can they really be blamed for taking the spies at their word, with their exaggerated stories of the giants? Did they merit such drastic punishment?

Meanwhile, what of Zipporah, who bravely defended Moses against Yahweh's attempt to murder him? She bore a son, Gershom, but she is deprived of her husband by Yahweh. Moses is kept too busy continuously. What happened to Moses' sons? Surely the sons of such a great father should have received some recognition. Moses was a stranger in the land of Midian, hence the Gershon name (means 'stranger') he chose for his first son. But we have no further news of his family. Only that his tribe became the Levite priests, called Mushites.

Moses is the really outstanding, heroic figure of the Bible – more than David, who is the hero for J and E and everybody else. We learn nothing from J of Moses' life as a prince of Egypt. We know little of his family background, except they were of the tribe of Levi. What happened to them afterwards? Why is it that we only learn about Aaron, his brother, when Moses needs help with his stutter? We need to know whether he really maintained contact with his family to learn that he was a Hebrew. How else could he become incensed at the treatment of his fellows?

But this undoubtedly is J's greatest of all stories. He weaves his plot with unerring skill, and keeps our attention alive and concentrated from the beginning. Quiet and modest Moses appears throughout, keeping his patience all those weary years with his unruly, quarrelsome, often frightened and hysterical, but always, always grumbling people. He loses his wonderful patience only twice – once when he strikes the rock to draw forth water without recognition publicly of the power of Yahweh, under the continuous harassment of his impatient, selfish people. Worse, however, when he descends from Sinai, proudly bearing his precious tablets, inscribed by Yahweh himself, to be confronted by the dancing, singing, unspeakably behaving mob around Aaron's golden calf. Is it any wonder he smashes the tablets and the golden calf? It would not have been surprising had he smashed most of the miscreants. But he recovered and pleaded for them, like the truly great, compassionate leader he was, when Yahweh wished to destroy them all. Truly there was none like him.

Why then was Moses pushed to one side in the history of the Bible, and well-nigh neglected and forgotten, in place of those much later colourful heroes, like David and Solomon? If Abraham and the Patriarchs were regarded as the original founders of the Jewish nation, who later evolved (though I believe that we must go right back to the ancient Hibarus and the Ibri), then surely it was Moses who really laid the foundations of Israel. Without his leadership, they would not have escaped those punishing years of the deadly burden of bondage, tantamount finally to slavery, in their enemy's power, until they too vanished down the vortex of history, condemned for their infamous torture of an innocent people, as a prime example of 'man's inhumanity to man'.

Moses emerges as the Israelites' greatest rescuer and leader. He must have kept records and accounts, lists of the tribes and their members, noting down major events and battles, even minor incidents and encounters. Surely he (or Aaron) will have entered the commands and punishments of Yahweh, and striking situations like Mount Sinai, major and minor revolts, certainly the horrific reaction of the people at the reports of the spies from their exploration of Canaan. Whether he, too, was principally the creation of J and E and D, followed by many other writers – perhaps, after all, a figment of J's imagination, as some still claim – remains to be proven.

Some day archaeologists may be fortunate to discover tablets, scrolls, records (such as those kept profusely by the Sumerians) to expose the truth of this period, which has so excited world interest for thousands of years. The great rescue and pilgrimage of a great multitude of people, eventually growing into millions on their way to development into a great nation. This amazing story, which has stirred the imagination of century after century, must have been recorded in many different ways over those long, weary, 40 years of incomparable endurance and suffering, and in the years following. There must have been scribes to enter all these events in records yet to be revealed.

The burdens of this great leader must at times have been intolerable, especially when he had to bear the incessant chiding and threats of his Yahweh in addition to the daily round of grumbles, groans, and unceasing problems presented by this 'stiff-necked', obstinate, stubborn, wilful and often childish people. Keeping these fractious millions alive and well must have taken their toll, so that he had to appoint leaders under him, of 'tens of thousands' down to 'hundreds', with an overriding conference of elders to spread his burden. Those 40 years must have seemed an eternity, and a lesser man might well have longed to be free of them all. Yet he still wished to go on leading them into the Promised Land and beyond, until the final, callous, spurning dismissal by the Yahweh he had served so faithfully.

A perfect example of the hopeless situation Moses had to face arose when the people, tired of their unbroken, unchanging daily diet of this light, dewy-like substance called manna, demanded something more substantial, like meat. Moses really had to agree, knowing that more solid food was necessary to keep them alive, well and energetic, to stand up to their daily burdens, so he pleads their case to Yahweh: the people are always hungry and thirsty, lacking daily water and a more substantial diet. As usual Yahweh explodes into indignant reproval: 'Ye shall not eat one day, nor two days, nor five days, neither ten days, nor twenty days; but a whole month, until it come out at your nostrils, and it be loathsome unto you.' (Numbers 11:9-20) This was an unfeeling Yahweh, who did not seem to care for or consider his own created human beings and their physical needs. He was too much taken up with his own needs and their duties to him. Imagine the feelings and reactions of a father of a big, hungry family? It does not bear consideration.

Poor Moses not only had to put up with this intransigent, unruly great mass of people, but also with an impatient, recalcitrant Yahweh, whose ever-quick temper was set aflame by the smallest argument or deviation. No wonder the later rabbis decided that J's Yahweh had to be drastically changed and remade, softer, quieter, gentler and more distant, far removed from the irritations and dangerous questions, problems and sometimes unpleasing behaviour of his awkward, disobedient humans.

How cogent is Moses' diplomatic reply to Yahweh's hot temper: 'How long will this people affront me? I will put disease in front of them, erase their inheritance.' Wise Moses replies: 'Egypt will hear what you have done to the very people your power brought out from them. And then it will reach the inhabitants of the other land.'– in other words you will become a laughing stock as they mock your failure... end of argument. But Yahweh still had a last word, sending plague to kill off large numbers of the grumblers. And he did not forget or forgive Moses for preventing his latest attempt at mass slaughter.

J displays great skill in producing such variety of pictures in detail, to capture and hold the imagination of his readers. He, like later writers of world renown, was not to know that his work would be of such far-reaching consequence. If only it could have been preserved for us in its entirety, our concepts might well have been radically changed for all major religions, and so much war and fanaticism and strife avoided. The final cost of the Sinai disobedience was further years of suffering in that debilitating Wilderness, in order to be chastened, disciplined, hardened and fashioned into the final shape required, for their expected entry into the Promised Land. But for all those years of endurance there was to be no compensation, no final victory and entry into the Promised Land, only death assigned to all those who slaved in Egypt, still to suffer and be condemned to death, with all promises broken by a bitter

71

Yahweh, whose only concession was to allow their children to enter Canaan – without their parents. J was witnessing the disintegration of David's great empire, split asunder by Solomon's unworthy sons, with their ill-fated dual kingdoms. This must have coloured his own views and writing.

J was a weaver of ancient myth, folklore and fables, and yet a realist, who observed clearly the good and bad of the world around him, and sought the truth of the great events of the past. He had his own style and presentation, as may be gathered from those of his scrolls fortunately preserved for us. He was not a biblical author in the modern sense, and did not set out to write a Bible. Indeed it was some 600 years later before the first five books were produced. Our Bible, from which came later amended and even much altered editions, came into being after yet another spell of 600 years, re-written by the continuously arguing and debating rabbis of the second century AD, into the Middle Ages and on, moving ever further from the original. They were all too intent on removing or hiding all possible traces of its great originator, and his objective rendition of what he believed from his deep research and consideration, to be the realistic description of the 'Beginning', to which, after all, he was many centuries nearer than these later wiseacres. He was fully aware of the history and writings of neighbouring countries and their effect on his own people.

So much of his work and conclusions, and realistic presentation, did not suit the subjective, self-seeking, power-hungry Aaronite priests who followed hundreds of years later, that they could not allow it to remain in its original form. Especially J's Yahweh who, for their taste, had to be radically changed in almost every respect into their desired form, far removed from the sight of and personal contact with humans. They were intent upon producing a changed, quiet, matured Yahweh in

72

their own desired form, to be presented to their people by them, as their only contact henceforth with their God, Adonai, through his appointed priests. So it has continued.

If J is therefore to be cast aside into limbo with his first biblical rendering, into an unknown grave like his Moses, who then are we to believe? The unique originator, or the self-centred priests who followed, more intent on winning their internecine struggles for supremacy between Mushites and Aaronites, who hated each other, could never work in harmony for the good of their people (similar to modern priestly antagonisms), until finally both were cast aside? It was the Redactor, thought to be Ezra himself, who finally put an end to their squabbling and rewriting different versions. About 400 BC, he made a composite selection of old and new from all their various scripts, favouring P more than J/E, being himself an Aaronite priest. This edition was generally accepted through the centuries, until the rabbis began a massive attack, especially on J, thereby changing J's original version, principally his anthropomorphic Yahweh, now completely 'done over'. Their version became the foundation of modern Judaism – also Christianity and Islam. But all three major religions are content to trace their roots and origin back to Abraham, 'Father of ALL Nations'.

However, in the light of our present knowledge and archaeological discoveries, we now need to go right back to the origins of the Beginning, and start afresh from there with all possible ancient tablets and scrolls. Only there may the truth be revealed as to what is fact, and what fiction in those ancient times, and how much of the Bible and other religious scripts and versions may be believed or were simply the products of skilful imaginative writing.

J was an objective historian with no adherence to any priestly or other sect. He set out to relate the story of the Beginning of the world as he visualised it, and the various influences brought to bear, including all the different concepts of its Creator, with possibly a Supreme Spirit overall, and the development especially of the human beings now created. He saw beyond the confines of Rehoboam's court to the fast-expanding world beyond, hungry for knowledge and insight (*vide* Darius, Cyrus, Artaxerxes), into the purpose and meaning of life. Far beyond his own ability to comprehend, when he first set pen to papyrus – even his own precious talent.

He did not seek the nascent meaning of the Beginning. His stories are a mixture of folklore and his own real belief, culled from research into the ancient past and his primitive forbears and their gods, who often assumed human form, ways and behaviour. He is not a complete believer and follower of Yahweh, but seeks to learn to comprehend him from every strength and weakness. Yahweh is not accepted as perfection by later priestly writers. J's concept is much closer to mankind, sharing some of its weaknesses, as well as his own ultimate strength and authority. Yahweh is in keeping with the primitive gods who were human-like though supernatural, such as Marduk, supremo of the Babylonian gods.

J is a prose poet with an exuberance of invention and language, with remarkable word fluency, and always clearly comprehensive. He describes Jacob's unceasing trials, from his first struggle against his brother's seniority, commencing in the womb with that sensational word picture of Jacob clutching Esau's heel so as not to be left behind, to his final reunion with his long-lost favourite son, Joseph. Everything comes hard to Jacob, who has to endure 14 years' hard labour to win his beloved Rachel. But he will not be beaten, even by Yahweh's angel, who engages him in mortal combat and

74

renames him Israel, thus setting him at last on his true mission in life, the foundation of a great nation.

That is an example of J's philosophy of life, of human suffering and lasting endurance, courage and hope right to the end. He is not a moralist, nor unquestioning of his own delineation of Yahweh from all angles. He does not condemn, but portrays his characters with deliberate clarity. His Moses is an undoubted leader, yet modest and, at first, self-effacing. J shows us first Moses' personal weaknesses and lack of belief in himself, then gradually growing in strength before our eyes, achieving full manhood in his confrontations with Pharaoh. Finally, taking command of that huge mixed mass of ex-slaves, over 600,000 men with all their women, children and grandparents, all their various possessions, including cattle, goats and birds. What man would not flinch from undertaking such a terrifying mission?

Babel was for J simply the overall, joint community's efforts to make it easier for Yahweh to descend to meet and mix with mankind. It is a good example of the simplicity of outlook of people at that time. Similar stories and like desires have been found with the Incas and Aztecs as well as Egyptians, Assyrians, Babylonians who built towers, pyramids and ziggurats, to make a pathway to heaven. Is there not a similar picture in Genesis 28:12: 'And he dreamed and behold a ladder set up on the earth, and the top of it reached to heaven; and behold the angels of God ascending and descending on it.' Jacob called the place Beth-el. But here Yahweh construes the building of the tower as humans' attempt to invade his kingdom. So he makes mischief to cause confusion of tongues, resulting in misunderstandings, and the collapse of this human enterprise. Yahweh feels his own power strengthened by division of his humans – possibly worrying about the problems their combined strength might cause him. Another

75

example of J's complex thinking, resolved in a tale of ironic humour at the height of man's ambition.

But Moses is J's final great heroic leader, suffering all manner of complicated daily problems, irritations and upsets from this heterogeneous mass forced by Yahweh into his care. He suffers almost equally from Yahweh's demands and outbursts, and murderous threats and deadly punishments, until he is summoned to that fateful meeting on Mount Sinai. There he receives the ten basic Commandments, to be his people's eternal guidance. The momentous confrontation with Yahweh is followed by the revolting scene that meets him on his joyful descent!

Here J is at his greatest scene-painting: contrast Moses raised above the earth, to the momentous personal meeting with Yahweh atop the mountain peak (as it were, the nearest point to heaven), descending imbued with heavenly grace, with Yahweh's own inscribed Tablets of the Law held aloft – only to encounter the vile scene of his untrustworthy, sinful people (led by his brother Aaron), worshipping and cavorting around their new-cast golden image, in direct defiance of Yahweh, a scene of degrading lust and depravity. What a fitting gesture of Moses, hurling down Yahweh's personal gift to his Children of Israel, to be smashed on the ground, pounded into dust, mixed with water and poured down their libellous and licentious throats. This is J at his most vivid, with a masterly portrayal of an unforgettable scene that will live for ever in all biblical records and paintings by great artists. The almost unbearable contrast between the extremes of good and evil. The continuation of mankind's fall to temptation inherited from Eden.

J and the TORAH (Will of God), the LAW

J does not foresee the future growth of Judaism, nor the effect his portrayal of Yahweh will have on the later priestly writers. The great rabbis and learned teachers, like Hillel and Akiba, served a merciful, spiritual monotheistic God, very different from J's manlike Yahweh. But there were also many differences arising between the rabbis and teachers and interpreters of the Bible. They all had one thing in common: all were intent on tearing J apart, as unsuitable for all their individual renderings and interpretations as priests. It matters not that they owed their very presence, rank and fame to this unique, original, unknown figure who emerged in the 10th century BC from the unwritten background of ancient history and their forbears, to write the very first edition of the opening Books of the Old ('Original') Testament. They even forbade any future mention of Yahweh, treating it almost as an unforgivable sin.

Who were they to decry and seek to expunge their great ancestor, known simply as J because he came from David's tribe of Judah, and wrote from his Holy City of Jerusalem? Vilify him they might, yet they are forced to accept much of layman J's original version, as still holding good. In the very same way that E and P and D and finally the Redactor, all bent on changing J's script to suit their own ends, had to accept the majority of his work, for they had none of them, nor yet these later argumentative rabbis, the wit or ability to gainsay or substitute his skilful production.

In fact it all seems to be concentrated in their major attacks on J's original rendering of the supernatural, monotheistic God Yahweh. Before his interpretation there were only the ancient gods of nature, the elements and household gods, *inter alia*. Suddenly there arises this unknown figure who writes down, seemingly for the first time ever, a really valid version

77

of what transpired 'In the Beginning' of this world of earth, sea and heaven, of man's first appearance and the consequences. Looking back through all the centuries over nearly 6000 years, little has changed except the delineation of Yahweh and the change forced by the priests to Adonai, interpreted now in modern form as: the Lord or Jehovah. How J would have been amused. To him Lord (as also to most people today), meant Lord and master, male head of the family, village, community, lord of an estate – but never would he have reduced the value of his YHVH to such lower human title. Sarai calls Abraham 'My Lord', as title of husband and head of the family. But she would never have addressed or spoken of Yahweh on that lower level.

So who is to judge? Here is an extract by Bloom and Rosenberg from J's original Creation:

'Yahweh shaped an earthling from clay of this earth, and blew into his nostrils the wind of life. Now look: man becomes a creature of the flesh.'
'As you sow, the sweat of your face, so will you reap your bread, till you return to earth, from it you were taken. Dust you are so dust you return.'

That was written by this unknown scribe of about 920 BC. Can we fault it today, when we still quote him 'dust to dust'? What matter if we have been able to suggest his sources? All writers, great and small, must derive their knowledge and inspiration from previous sources, study, research. What finally emerges from the melting pot of all their knowledge gained of the past, cooked in their own personal cauldron until it reaches white heat, and comes forth as their personal inspiration, is often the dynamic production of many of the world's greatest minds and authors, ancient and modern. We may differ in our individual translation or interpretation, but

78

we are all prepared, willingly and happily, to acknowledge and rejoice in such productions. Thus did Shakespeare delve into history, even to the Bible, to produce his outstanding characterisations of great figures and events of the past.

Not so, these eminent priests and churchmen. This layman's hard, tough, demanding Yahweh cannot be allowed to be so interpreted to the people. He must be changed to suit their interests and become born again as our 'Lord God on High', way up in his Heaven, far above the ordinary people – a spirit, unknown, unseen, whose commands, wishes and admonishments may best be interpreted by his chosen (?) priests and earthly interpreters to the people. So they feel free to pass judgements, moralise, instruct, punish, raise armies of followers for one personal formation or another, to follow their instructions and their form of faith, often leading to fanaticism and assassinations and torture or murder in different forms. Abraham and Moses must turn in their graves at such behaviour, misconceived power struggles and selfish interpretation of the descendants of Moses' own tribe, whom he made priests, to care for and serve his people.

Returning to J: he does not pass personal judgement, nor does he become personally involved (as do so many of these new interpreters of the Bible). He remains objective and does not give personal criticism. He implies moral philosophies in his delineation of characters, whether Cain or Solomon or the sad division in his own time of David's great kingdom into Israel and Judah, leaving us to conclude the fate of the 'house divided'. He reveals the archaic form of Judaism (now mainly lost), as the background of the birth, growth and development of the new.

He remains the greatest writer and portrayer of the Old Testament. His humour, his incisive style and word usage, creating

79

colourful character sketches in few words, with clear, bold presentation, are unequalled amongst the world's greatest writers. There is every facet of human life and experience within his chapters: love, hate, romance, rape, revenge, worship, rebellion, murder, assassination; deep plots leading to battles and wars, spies and agents, detectives, policing, judgements and punishments – all are there to enjoy in J's presentation of his rich tapestry.

His insight into human nature compares with the world's greatest authors. J was a true democrat, almost conversing with us in matter-of-fact tones. He reduces everybody to the same level, be they kings or leaders, with the same human understanding of the situation and actions of each of his characters, drawn with such skill that we accept his revealing definitions, without even being aware of the inferences he persuades us to draw. The mark of the naturally great writer. His Yahweh is the most dynamic of gods, with whom none of the ancient can compare, but remains unpredictable. But none of J's original deity is now left – altered, changed and finally obliterated by priests out of all recognition from J's original texts.

Yet J's vision of the Creation came to dominate Judaism, as also his portrayal of the men and women of all ranks and situations as he sets them all before us. He should be acknowledged even now by all religions, priests and churches, and by all lay people, as the greatest of all biblical authors and writers. As the Bible aptly says: 'And there was none like unto him, and there was none came after like him.'

3

J's YAHWEH

The anthropomorphic God, as portrayed by J in 920 BC, deeming him similar to man: 'Let us make man in our own image, after our likeness.' (Genesis 1:24) Yahweh creates man, but remains different from him. Yet at times he displays an almost humanlike personality. He is temperamental and ever-demanding, exploding into instant anger when thwarted or disobeyed, especially by those worshipping 'false gods'. His judgements are instantaneous, allowing no defence nor mitigation, and are totally without consideration or mercy. Punishments are usually harsh, out of proportion to the fault, error or crime committed, leading to slavery or even death of large numbers of innocents, condemned with the guilty.

J's Yahweh is very close to the Sumerian, Akkadian and Babylonian concept of their gods. They often took human form and attitudes like people, adopting similar behaviour, with manlike emotions, rages, jealousies and demands. Though possessed of supernatural powers, they interfered in human affairs in arbitrary ways. Yahweh differs only as the first and sole monotheistic god, jealous of his supreme power over his creatures, and demanding total affinity, worship and obedience.

Good, honest, long-suffering Job, a quiet, well-behaved, patient, God-fearing man, is subjected to the most heart-rending agonies for no valid reason. Simply because Yahweh succumbs to Satan's cunning wager, thereby reducing Himself to the level of the evil one, Baal-zebub (became Beelzebub – the Devil: Lord of the Flies). The whole episode is obviously myth and a folklore tale, but starkly revealing of Yahweh's worldliness and insensitivity to human feelings. He has his favourites, Abraham and David above all, then Sarah, Jacob, Joseph, Rachel, Ruth and Esther. Personal meetings take place with Adam and Eve, Abram, Jacob and of course Moses, most of all. He is even prepared to argue with Sarah, and later haggle with Abraham on the way to destroy sinful Sodom and Gomorrah. He inspires mixed emotions, principally fear.

It is only those of extra strength and leadership and firm belief who truly admire and worship Yahweh as their supreme leader: 'He who must be obeyed'. He will allow no arguments or backsliding. He is like man and like other gods in their material form. But he rises above them all and their supernatural powers. Insensitive, without mercy or compunction, he shows no feelings or forgiveness, no mercy for repentance, and is totally subjective and self-concerned until the arrival of the Prophets, who begin to change his image in the eyes and thoughts of his people.

Moses his greatest, most patient, long-suffering, chosen leader, and a man of sterling character, modest, impersonal, dedicated to his onerous, gigantic task, but ever his faithful servant, is treated worst of all. From the very commencement of his frightening mission, having been powerfully persuaded by Yahweh (who will not take no for an answer, despite Moses' plea that he is unworthy for such a task, and stutters into the bargain), Moses is in deadly trouble. Yahweh, for no given reason, sends his messengers to kill Moses. It is only the courageous intervention of his wife Zipporah, which saves him. Yahweh treats him roughly all the way through those long-suffering 40 years in the vast Wilderness, finally condemning him to die deprived of his well-earned, long desired reward of leading his people into the Promised Land. Yahweh kills him off quickly and buries him secretly in an unknown, unmarked grave, beyond human ken. Perhaps Yahweh feared it might become a hallowed spot, visited by future generations as a martyr's grave, which it certainly would have been. There could be no possible reason for such diabolical, unworthy treatment of a man still fit and alert in his mind and body. This final ignominy is unaccountable, and destroys any understanding one might seek of J's real concept of his most important figure.

Yahweh's lack of patience, tolerance and mercy rapidly increases throughout Exodus, and is lost altogether at Mount Sinai. His irritability grows as his 'Children of Israel' make their slow progress through that desolate Wilderness of Zin. Their sulks, groans, grumbles and waywardness, and spasmodic transgressions, turn him into a most hot-tempered, violent deity. Their hunger for more substantial food than the daily dose of manna, drives them to demand meat. Yahweh, obviously unconcerned and unfeeling about their daily diet and continuous lack of water and real sustenance, turns his wrath upon them, that they should dare to ask for more! He feeds them nothing but meat in the form of droves of quail for every meal, day after day, until it comes out of their nostrils, and they are sickened of it. Peculiar conduct for the concerned, feeling father of such a huge family! Worst of all, they are now condemned to die in the Wilderness before entry to the Promised Land – a 'punishment greater than the crime'. But, like Sumerian gods, Yahweh shows no parental personal feelings, or emotions of love and pity. He is an extremist, with no soft core. Even when making them sick with his overdose of meat, he still cannot resist his long-held habit of sending plagues to destroy them, until once again persuaded by Moses to desist this heartless killing of his creatures.

One asks what crime could be so heinous, as to rob them of their long-fought, and long-suffered reward for 40 years of nomadic life, forced upon them by a seemingly unfeeling, intolerant Yahweh whose temper is always on a short fuse, ready to blow up for the slightest argument, mishap or misdemeanour. This reward has been promised and confirmed continuously from Abraham onwards. Like all his promises this, his greatest, regularly repeated, is now to be finally broken, and their hard-earned reward snatched away at the very end of their travails. After hundreds of years of hard bondage under harsh Pharaohs and bullying Egyptian taskmasters, they now have to learn new modes of behaviour, whilst suffering the hardships of that endless, arid desert land. Despite it all, they hugged to their breasts the promised reward – their crock of gold at the end, to enter and enjoy this Promised Land of 'milk and honey'.

We are not told how, when or where they met their ignominious deaths. Yahweh's palate for destruction of his own human creatures kills off countless numbers of his 'children' from the Flood to this final agony before the entry to the 'Promised Land'. Their only consolation is that their children (or possibly grandchildren) will be allowed to enter without their parents, having been duly trained in arms for the forthcoming hard battles against many foes, as they seek to cross Canaan. Nothing comes easily from Yahweh, who habitually makes them pay heavily for their pleasures. At the same time demanding their incessant worship of him 'above all other gods', and instant obedience to his commands and complete acquiescence to his wishes. Woe betide any who fall by the wayside or transgress or dare to complain, or, worst of all, fail to acknowledge him daily as Supremo, above all other gods as 'He who must be obeyed' – and that on the instant.

Throughout the Bible, it seems that Moses is reduced in size and value, compared with Yahweh's and everybody's hero, David. Surely Moses has no equal anywhere in the world, considering the enormous task he undertook from his quiet life as a shepherd with his adopted Midian family of Jethro, priest, farmer and later his adviser. To leave wife and family and a peaceful, pleasant existence, to undertake a mission of such gigantic measure, demands the courage, patience, and physical and mental strength of heroes. This he proved in full measure, not only enduring all the manifold, ever-increasing problems of his recalcitrant people, but also patiently accepting the flood of daily orders, commands and tantrums of his overall commander, Yahweh, who had suddenly erupted into his life. Now implacably forcing him, heedless of any possibility of a refusal, to undertake this perilous mission, for which he felt himself completely unfitted.

First Moses had to undertake the enormous hazardous task of bearding harsh Pharaoh, Rameses II in his Palace, from which he had been forced to flee for his life, after killing the Egyptian taskmaster who was bullying and beating a Hebrew slave. Imagine his feelings at having to face again the brutal monarch who sought his death. It must have taken enormous courage to make his firm demands, on behalf of this unknown Hebrew God Yahweh, to release all the Hebrews completely from slavery. Laughed at and taunted by Pharaoh and his entourage, Moses gathered up his courage and firm stature, defying Pharaoh and proving that his one god Yahweh was greater than all the Egyptian gods, magicians and sorcerers. Finally he prevailed, and set forth with this motley collection of over 600,000 men with their women and children, cattle and all their belongings, staggering out of hated Egypt, and making their way en masse towards the Sea of Reeds. What a mass it must have been to move somehow towards that sea. They desperately needed Yahweh's mist behind them to confuse the revengeful Egyptian forces.

After such travails Moses now has to keep this long, weary multitude of old and young, fit and infirm, moving as fast as possible, fearing pursuit from Pharaoh's chariots. It is worthy of a chapter to itself to recount all those adventures, the miraculous crossing of the Red Sea, and Yahweh's drowning of all Pharaoh's chariots and warriors in the returning tide, to the first encampment at Succoth. It must have been a truly tremendous task, which Moses saw through with great courage and aplomb, fast acquiring the power of command and guidance. He even composed a song of deliverance in praise of Yahweh, unable to foresee all his travails in the long, weary years ahead.

Yahweh pressed Moses into this awesome mission, which he carried out to perfection, without even trusting him at first to carry it out alone. But Moses grew daily in stature and confidence. Without him, those fractious, undisciplined ex-slaves, suddenly released from long-suffering bondage, would surely have perished long since, in that desolate vast desert Wilderness. Yahweh alone would not have put up with them for long. He sought to destroy them utterly on repeated occasions. But Moses held them firmly, trained and disciplined them, appointed leaders over each tribe, taught them the arts of war (learnt as an Egyptian Prince), trained his own tribe of Levi to produce priests to minister to the people, and teach them the duties of their religion and personal welfare.... What a gigantic task perpetually encompassing him all round. Especially as they grew and multiplied, despite their nomadic wanderings. Their numbers swelled to over 2 million souls in his care. Whoever has had to face such a task throughout world history? Moses taught them the laws of conduct, hygiene and general behaviour and discipline. He acted as father, mother and nurse, even protecting them many times from Yahweh.

What of Yahweh, whilst Moses was carrying out his task, greater than all those of Hercules? Was he encouraging Moses, supporting, helping in every way possible, such as finding places to rest, food and water. Oh no – he was ever at Moses' shoulder, criticising, commanding, stipulating, issuing fresh instructions, some quite impossible to carry out in those desert conditions. Always ready to pounce on any deviation, Yahweh grew daily more irritated by the irresponsible conduct of these newly released ex-slaves. His demands on Moses and the people grew ever more severe, and his punishments steadily more harsh and intemperate. The death-wish of the Flood in Genesis was revived often during those long, weary 40 years. So that in addition to his daily burdens with the people, Moses had to cope with an irritable, hot tempered, ever-demanding Yahweh, meting out harsh punishments like plagues, causing death, opening the ground to swallow up miscreants or rebels. His death-wish grew ever stronger, reaching its zenith at Mount Sinai. It was the extra task of wise, patient Moses, quietly to reduce that hot-temper, talk him round and plead forgiveness for his wayward people. If ever there were a man worthy of the title of Hebrew Saint, it was Moses.

Yahweh calls himself a 'Jealous God', meaning jealous of his sole monotheistic rôle and, at the same time, zealous in protection of his rights against any turning away of his creatures, to worship 'false gods'. He grants the power of blessing (also conveying inheritance rights, so important for the power of the family). This provokes the continuous desire and struggle for possession of this power, as exemplified in the family struggles of Jacob, David, Ishmael and Solomon.

J's Yahweh favoured above all his women leading characters: Sarah, Rebecca, Rachel, Tamar, Ruth, Zipporah, Bathsheba, Esther – many of whom came from outside the Israelites and their special faith. There was Ruth the Moabite and Tamar the Canaanite, from both of whom came eventually David, the dynamic hero of the Jewish Bible. There was no Hebrew law against mixed marriages. Indeed the Hebrews (or Ibri) came originally from the ancient Hibaru, a composite mix of different nomadic groups. So men were accustomed to seek wives from 'outside', who willingly conformed to the faith and customs of their husbands. It was King Josiah who was the first to seek (but in vain), to stop such intermingling. 'Twas ever thus.

These women were often tougher, more courageous and resilient than their menfolk, supporting, defending and fighting for them: Zipporah defended Moses against the would-be assassins sent by Yahweh; Rachel supported compliant Jacob against her cunning father Laban, taking his treasured household gods in compensation for her lack of dowry from the greedy, wily fellow; Tamar determined to fight her way into her new family, despite the early death of her weakling husbands who could not give her sons, with the dynamic courage to win her cause; Sarai, barren at 90, becomes jealous and more determined when her handmaid Hagar (given by her as compensation to Abraham) produces son Ishmael, fathered by Abraham. She forces Yahweh to keep his promise and intercede on her behalf to produce Isaac, by using her ultimate weapon of mockery which certainly seemed to sting Yahweh into action, if only to prove her wrong.

J's Yahweh changes as the story progresses. He becomes a rather different deity from our first introduction by J, though his dealings remain ever harsh with any who fail to obey his commandments or, worse still, dare to worship 'graven images'. But this new version has now become more of a dynamic leader, who chooses Moses, organises the Exodus, produces terrible plagues, kills off all Egyptian first-born sons, including Pharaoh's. He makes another of his Covenants with the leaders and elders at Sinai – only to revert to the temperamental, harsh punisher, as his patience is sorely tried when his named 'Children of Israel' act like mischievous offspring. He now becomes the most uncaring and ungrateful Yahweh, when he chooses to condemn his ever-faithful, long-serving leader Moses to an ignominious death for specious unworthy reason, just before the actual entry into the Promised Land, in a secret, unmarked grave. Surely one of the worst examples of history of palpable ingratitude for the 40-year-long, enduring patient leadership of a loyal, trustworthy servant. But this Yahweh was in the mould of those ancient gods and supernaturals with images of stone, who could not share the feelings and sufferings of mankind.

No wonder later writers decided to change the image of this all-too-anthropomorphic Yahweh. They were all priests, seeking to emphasise religion as their main objective, whereas J was not a priest. He was a layman and not a religious writer. That was a major difference between him, the originator, and his successors. He was more interested in the study of human conduct, so his views differed sharply from his priestly successors. He was essentially a storyteller and raconteur, who loved to portray individual characters and their reactions to the situations in which they found themselves or created. Especially with his portrayal of Yahweh (influenced by the ancient gods and their conduct, especially those of nature like the greatest character of the Bull, who ruled over nature with much noise, bellowing and clashing of hooves, with cohort Astarte). The Bull became Baal and was still worshipped in the majority of countries around them. J's Yahweh was manlike with some of man's worst features, but as Abram's El was much nearer to Baal even than some of his subjects. J has no equal in portraying the psychology of Yahweh, and all his other characters, with a few deft touches.

J shows much originality and ironic humour in his storytelling (unlike the priests who were all deadly serious and unflinching), ranking with the greatest world authors. What more enjoyable ironic comedy than pompous philosopher Balaam, setting out on his faithful ass to assist Barak, the Moabite chief, by cursing the feared Israelites. Three times he fails to see Yahweh's angel blocking his path with drawn sword. But the donkey sees him and steps out of the way, to be whipped back onto the road, until the ass speaks out to reprimand Balaam – who then notices the angel and gets the message. He now refuses to curse, but instead blesses the Israelites and prophesies the defeat of the Moabites:

> 'How goodly are thy tents, O Jacob, Thy dwellings, O Israel.'

Such a comic tale, worthy of inclusion in Chaucer's *Canterbury Tales*. It has been told and retold through all generations to this day, as an enjoyable ingot of biblical history. The laughter is good medicine, to cure much disbelief and lighten so many tragic stories, like that of the moral degradation of Shittim: 'As Israel is yoked there, embracing Baal-peor, Yahweh is inflamed.' He cries: 'Round up the heads of the people. Hang them before Yahweh in broad daylight, until Yahweh's anger is burned away from Israel.' Because the Israelites have cavorted with the daughters of Moab, who are descended from Lot's illicit offspring. Now, having also worshipped their false gods (the most heinous crime against Yahweh), they must be punished publicly and decisively.

J is not afraid to reveal Yahweh's weaknesses, lack of consideration or sympathy and hot, intemperate rages, followed by extreme harsh punishment. But later writers, especially P and R (both from priestly Aaronite backgrounds), differ sharply in their attitude to Yahweh. Over the intervening hundreds of years, their attitudes and priestly mode of thinking changed radically. Their Yahweh remains a 'Jealous God', threatening dire punishment to those who break his Laws and Commandments. But he now becomes distant, in some respects quite different: 'merciful, patient, tolerant, forgiving'. J would be quite unable to recognise this Yahweh, so changed from his original concept, inherited from his ancestors and neighbours, such as Bull-el, the forceful, ever-demanding god of creation, subject to awful rages and stamping of hooves to make the very earth tremble. But it was the Prophets who really changed and softened Yahweh's image.

J's original Yahweh says 'I am who I am' – 'I will be what I will be' (Exodus 37). He is not prepared to go into details but prefers to indicate that he is all-powerful, able to be and do whatever he chooses. However, he states clearly that he is a 'jealous God' and will brook no turning aside by any of his people, high or low, to seek comfort from graven images (who, after all, cannot answer back or actually threaten dire punishment for the slightest wrong). For these ancient ancestors were frail in such matters – like so many even now, who turn aside to worship false gods like Mammon, or even graven images to be found inside and outside our churches and in many homes. The priests did not disagree, they simply wished to take over the rôle themselves as Yahweh's priestly instruments and voice. The early Yahweh as portrayed by J was intolerant of disloyalty and disobedience, rarely showing active concern for his people, yet unforgiving of failure to obey, and capable of harsh, sometimes deadly punishment. His was rule by fear and threats, under the whiplash of dire results.

At the same time Yahweh pronounces himself a 'Holy God', 'The Holy One', and Israel, his Creation, is to be a 'Holy Nation' (Exodus 199). Yahweh expresses this in a Covenant in Exodus 6:7: 'I will take you for my people and I will be your God.' The Ten Commandments begin: 'I am the Lord your God, who brought you out of the Land of Egypt, out of the house of bondage.' This must be acceptable to all three faiths alike: Jewish, Christian and Muslim. However, believers of all three faiths now prefer an invisible Yahweh, way above the clouds, as a distant spirit, even when they may be suffering under a tyrant king or tough dictator. So far have we been seduced from J's original Yahweh, who was always close to mankind and involved at all times, though often to human discomfort. A debatable point, for present worshippers have no concept of the ancient Yahweh, as first revealed by the original creator of the Beginning.

Yahweh remains, from J to the Redactor, a personality of extraordinarily complex nature. Though later Jewish theology dispenses with the anthropomorphic, it is still retained in both Christian and Muslim theology. J never actually describes Yahweh, but he ensures that we always feel his presence implied, as he 'overheard' sister Miriam and brother Aaron gossiping about Moses and his wife. As a supreme writer and teller of tales, J compels us to envisage his characters and scenes, often vividly, without seeing them. Yahweh warns Moses to get back down the mountain, for his people are corruptly worshipping a golden calf. He always knows what is going on, yet allows it to happen and then punishes the culprits and their associates.

Yet with all the alterations and 'improvements' made by priests and rabbis, it is curiously significant that the very prayers and psalms heard in our churches and other places of worship, still bear a strong resemblance to, often a direct repeat of those original prayers of Moses and Aaron, David with his glorious Psalms, and the Patriarchs.

Finally, it must be left to individuals to judge and make up their own minds, casting aside all else, until the real Prophets return, to quote the full truth and guide us all to a better future. The fact remains that after all these past thousands of years, mankind has not yet been able to dispense with wars, violence and extremes (like fanaticism), and learn to live together in peace, trust and harmony. Are we better off in faith, goodwill and cooperation now, with all our marvellous, modern, technical inventions, than J's people and their Yahweh?

No pagan god fully corresponded to Yahweh who, unlike them, was not just a power in nature. Dynamic vitality is the prime characeristic of J's Yahweh. He has no specific gender, but is a deity of pure will and wilfulness. The ancient Yahweh was a natural warrior god, without holiness and pure goodness, but he does have his own truth and forms of justice, severe though they may be. At Creation, he says: 'Be like me, breathe with my breath.' But at Sinai he says: 'Don't you dare be too like me!' He was bound up with his Creation, for good or ill, and his people, whatever punishment they might receive, held on tenaciously to their own special religion in exile, reinforcing their national identity. Lamentations and Psalm 137 witness their longing for home and Jerusalem – a longing that expresses itself through every century following. The end of Isaiah and the Book of Ezekiel reflect the exiles' life, trapped in Babylon: 'How shall we sing a song of Yahweh on foreign soil?' They even questioned their Yahweh, who had allowed this to happen. Their answer came: it was their own fault for failing to keep their Covenant.

But these were humans, created by Yahweh with all their

93

weaknesses but still with free will. They are his creatures, so how can he blame them for being human? After all, it was he who failed and left them, not they who left him. He seems unable to understand their human failings, and cannot really expect everyone to be a David. No wonder they fear his violent, excessive anger and severe punishment. So they turn for solace and comfort to the pagan gods like Baal and Astarte who, after all, are graven images and cannot answer back or punish them. Even David and Solomon included Baal in the names of their children.

The question remains: how much of J's Yahweh was inherited from the ancient gods of his ancestors? How much of J's fertile imagination and innovative mind produced those awe-inspiring portrayals of Yahweh? Or how much more reliable are the watered-down versions of the priestly scribes who followed J hundreds of years later? Or the final version of the Redactor, over 500 years after J, with its scrambled final concoction – yet still having to retain much of the old, original J? How can the final, decimated and remoulded version of the learned rabbis of the second century AD be possibly believed as the only TRUE version, or that of the new version of the Gospels?

The combination of scientists' timing and dating, with archae-ologists' latest fresh discoveries of definite evidence of our ancient ancestors, must combine to allow us insight into the really factual situation of the early biblical era, to learn and decide for ourselves what really happened at the Beginning of our world and just who was this original Creator, whether Yahweh, Adonai or Jehovah, or this unknown Supreme Spirit who controls the stars, planets, heavens and our little world beyond our grasp.

4

JUDEA

Palestine was a small country in size but of great significance in its growth in importance, from about 3500 BC. Its geographical location was significant, lying between three main areas of the Near East, through which flowed the mainstream of traffic of traders, armies and cultural influences:

1) The Delta along the Nile, protecting Egypt's safety by huge deserts.
2) Between the Tigris and Euphrates rivers occupied by the great conglomeration of Sumerians, Assyrians, Persians, Akkadians, Amorites, Kassites, with Babylonians on the mountains.
3) The area west of the river Jordan. North of Palestine (now Syria and Lebanon) lies Asia Minor, home of the Hittites. The Coastal Plain lies along the West with its ten natural harbours.

A great cleft divides the hills to west and east. The Jordan flows down to the Sea of Galilee, 695 feet below the Mediterranean and then 65 miles further to the lowest level of the Dead Sea. Finally Transjordan, rich farming country, containing Gilead, Moab and Amman.

Palestine lay 150 miles from Dan in the North to Beersheba in the south, between the great trade routes to Egypt, Africa and Arabia. Hence the greed and jealousy of all the large and

95

small groups around her. All busily attacking each other but all prepared to co-operate in attacking their common fierce enemy encroaching on all their borders; the Israelites, who occupied the western extremity, known as the 'Fertile Crescent'.

The major growth of populations and agriculture was due to the fruitful area of Mesopotamia lying between the two great rivers, Tigris and Euphrates. The Nile was responsible for the tremendous growth and strength of Egypt, the largest and most powerful country at that period of the Middle East, dominating others to gain important advantages in trade and products. Judea benefited from trade growth and the strength and vitality of her people, emerging from their nomadic origins, to become a strong farming, agricultural and industrial fruitful country. But she was never free from fierce battles from other countries, jealous of her success and seeking to win her trade benefits. Forced to fight continuously to maintain her area, Judea nevertheless, despite her many great victories, still had to suffer some defeats and humiliation, principally at the greedy hands of the Assyrians, Babylonians and Persians, who also kept fighting each other. So Judea was forced at times to serve different masters as a vassal state, or have her towns plundered and destroyed. No wonder they became such a strong, virile and energetic people, always alert and ready for war.

However, their nomadic roots still prevented them from becoming a closely knit, integrated and complete entity. When they split up into their 12 tribes, named after Jacob's sons, they remained separate entities, and only seemed to unite either at times of danger or war, or under a strong king or leader such as David, Solomon or Moses. There was a continuous, internecine struggle for predominance, and it took David, their greatest warrior leader, to weld them together into one great composite nation. Most of all, they were combined indissolubly in their abiding faith in one God, which divided them from all others who retained their primitive manifold gods and spirits. This monolithic faith became the seal of their combined strength. Whatever misfortunes they were forced to suffer through all their history, it is their undaunted faith in their One God which has enabled them to come back again and again through the worst horrors of war and torture, and even mass slaughter, with their eternal battle cry: 'Hear O Israel, the Lord our God, the Lord is One.'

They can rightly claim that their great faith, which they trace back to Abraham, dubbed 'Father of All Nations', has also been the foundation of Christianity and Islam; and Mohammed, their great prophet, was said to have been taught by rabbis. It is surely time now that these great nations, who alike worship the same basic God/Allah, should combine in their proper brotherhood (and sisterhood, since powerful women are again emerging as in the early biblical times), to their mutual benefit, in co-operation for peace and prosperity and total well-being. The foundations are already well laid. There is an abundance now of intelligence and developing education and ability to produce sufficient food and necessities of life. All it needs is the inspired leadership to combine with universal support, to lay these first essential foundation stones of eternal strength.

The awful fate staring us all right in the face, is now so imminent, with the development of the most terrible, devastating weapons of destruction threatening to lay waste the whole world at the touch of a few buttons. It is a threat of massive world-wide destruction, by nuclear and chemical weapons of unprecedented strength and reach. How can we, now so intelligent and with advanced, clear understanding, allow the days and weeks to slip by with even the smallest countries secretly arming themselves 'just in case', but knowing that the devastation, once the greatest and most terrible weapons are released, will render their expensive armaments useless.

Palestine, though once 'a land flowing with milk and honey', and well nurtured by the Israelis, who stored the seasonal rains and rebuilt and reworked the disused wells, with a system of canals to nourish the soil, was again devastated by war, burning and destruction. Land became waste, and desert was always ready to intrude and spoil the work of generations. The history of Palestine is older than usually estimated: Neanderthal skeletons have been discovered dating back some 40,000 years. Neolithic floors unearthed in Jericho, reputedly the Bible's oldest city, are of Middle Bronze Age (c 2000 BC).

Biblical dates are now generally accepted. Thus Abraham's move from Ur in Sumeria about 2200 BC began the Jewish faith in One God of all Nations. About 1000 years later, Moses commenced his greatest epic of the Exodus. In between unfolded the history and monotheistic religious growth of the Hebrews to become Israelites after Jacob. The Patriarchs carried this faith in Yahweh forward into the 400-year-long sojourn in Egypt, descending from Joseph's supreme position, through succeeding Pharaohs, to forced bondage with hard taskmasters, seeking not only to gain cheap labour, but somehow to reduce their ever-growing numbers. Even to the drastic resolution of murdering the first-born son of every family, to be followed by other sons, sparing only the daughters, whilst increasing their burdens of brick-making and building.

From this brutal slaughter of the babes came the epic story of Moses and the rescue of the Israelites by Exodus, from their arrival c 1650 BC under Joseph, to departure c 1220 BC.

Mysterious Moses became their great leader and wise, patient statesman, who ruled fairly, disciplined and taught this disorderly, unruly, disunited people with the aid (or hindrance) of an ever-watchful Yahweh, and setting an inspired yet modest example to all. Their origins are lost in the ancient history of the first primitive people who roamed nomadically, hunting and gathering food, and existing in small protected groups.

Known as Hibaru, one group emerged as Hebrews some 6000 years ago. First habitation areas were discovered in the basins of the great rivers, Tigris, Euphrates, Nile. They fashioned primitive, rough tools from stones, wood and animal bones. They worshipped Sun, Light, Fire, Nature and household gods. The Bull was the principal god of nature and fertilisation, Ashan and Astarte, goddess of grain and seed growth, Aleyan, bringer of rain, Anu and Lahar, the cattle god. All were worshipped and feared, so that sacrifices and celebrations were deemed necessary for propitiation of their gods.

These early Hebrews were a mixture of nomadic peoples, but once established, remained mostly within their own ethnic group. Descended from Shem, their physical characteristics were shared by all the Semites from the early Hebrews to the Assyrians, Akkadians, Babylonians, Phoenicians and Arabians. Their women were lauded as most beautiful of all, especially Rebecca, Rachel and Esther, who became Queen to King Ahasuerus, and thus saved her people from massacre planned by Haman. Their language, first oral and rhythmic, developed into written form with the first known alphabet of 22 letters without vowels about 3250 BC. They eventually became tribes based on the 12 sons of Jacob, with a council of elders, regarded as wise heads of family. This council acted as court of law and justice, dealing especially in urgent matters such as emergency, attack or defence. The authority of the family remained constant until Solomon developed the towns, attracting members of families (as Samuel had foretold), from farming and country life.

Samuel 8:10-20 warned of the problems kings would bring: 'And Samuel said... . 'He will take your sons... for his chariots and will appoint them captains over thousands and captains over fifties... to reap his harvest, make his instruments of war... . And he will take your daughters... to be cooks and bakers. And he will take your fields, and your vineyards... your menservants... the tenth of your sheep...' Nevertheless the people refused to listen to the voice of Samuel. Saul became their first warrior king, but the great responsibility proved too much for him. At first victorious, he later degenerated into madness and final defeat.

How different was young David. Mighty, clever warrior, winning battle after battle, subjugating all their foes, especially the Philistines. Accomplished musician and composer of songs and psalms, he was their outstanding statesman and acclaimed leader for 40 years, developing a widespread Empire, as never before nor since in Jewish history. He led the worship of Yahweh and danced his praise before the altar. No wonder he was the prime favourite of God and people, for he retained his charm and his regard for his people always. He sinned as other humans, in lusting after another man's wife, but accepted Nathan's rebuke humbly. Then he had to suffer the usual severe punishment of Yahweh, in the eventual loss of his ungrateful son Absalom, caught and killed in treasonable, armed rebellion against his father, after killing his own brother. Yet David mourned his loss, as a father: 'O my son Absalom, my son, my son Absalom! Would God I had died for thee, O Absalom.' (1 Samuel 18:33) A truly magnificent leader and democrat, who made his mark in history for all time (1000–961 BC). There never arose anyone to match him.

100

Unfortunately there was only the one David. His son Solomon (meaning 'peace', 961–922 BC), though he became a great king, began by slaying all his rivals. Forgiven by Yahweh because of his devout worship and his building of the first great Temple, he lived up to his name, attracting praise for his great wisdom and leadership in his major years. He exemplified the true value of law and order. He developed peace and friendship with other countries instead of war, and expanded trade and industry as never before. Great wealth increased as trade expanded. He built his own merchant fleet with the co-operation of David's good friend, King Hiram of Tyre. Hiram's Phoenician fleet served Solomon, bringing gold and metal from Ophir, and iron and copper from other countries, even tin from Cornwall. In addition there were jewels, apes and peacocks, rich materials and luxuries. He enjoyed a sybaritic life, marrying many wives, often diplomatically chosen, like the daughter of Pharaoh. But the biblical account of 700 wives and 300 concubines has been somewhat exaggerated. Brought down to figures of 68 and 30, it still seems a tremendous burden for one man. He indulged his foreign wives by allowing them to keep their own personal gods inside his palace, and was not averse to recognition of some of them himself, as was still the custom.

He made and spent his wealth lavishly. The Phoenicians built his Temple in seven years with all its ornate gold and silver work and gold plated cherubs. But his palace, many times bigger than the Temple, took over 13 years. It was of vast size, needed to house all his wives in luxury, as well as his concubines. Unfortunately, he gave them more of his time, neglecting not only his own regular worship, but also the care of his people. Becoming deep in debt, he had to trade cities to Hiram for payment. Desperate, he levied the highest burden of taxation on his people, in the form of a poll tax. The last straw, now desperately short of money, was forcing each and everyone to devote one month's free labour every year, an imposition greatly resented by all classes as unfair and unconstitutional.

His people became more and more discontented as he grew greedier and more selfish and sybaritic – so that his early death may have saved him from a revolution in 922. He had sadly neglected the education of his own sons in their duties, so they were not competent to take over his great kingdom. They quarrelled and split, with Jeroboam (922—901 BC), already a rebel, choosing the bigger slice of the north which he called Israel, taking with him ten of the tribes, nominating Samaria as his capital.

Rehoboam (922–915 BC) became King of Judah, with Jerusalem as his capital. The reign of Israel lasted 200 years, but little Judah continued until 587 BC. Then came the Babylonian Exile which lasted until 538 BC, over 50 long years. They all sadly missed Jerusalem and sang songs of mourning – but also blamed Yahweh for allowing all this terrible defeat and exile to happen, including the destruction of Jerusalem, David's great city, and Yahweh's own beautiful Temple, smashed and robbed. But there came no answer from Yahweh, who had abandoned them.

Those ancient nomad Hebrews never lost their attachment to their primitive gods, even when they accepted Yahweh, as sole God above all others. Moses was faced with the Golden Calf in defiance of his long, face-to-face discourse with their supreme 'Jealous God' Yahweh, who read into every disobedience a sign of their contempt for him, and punished them accordingly.

How then did Yahweh come into existence? No viable source or evidence is available other than the earlier anthropomorphic gods of Sumerians *et al.* A primitive god Yahu was found portrayed on pottery, dug up in Canaan in 1931, from the Bronze Age (c 3000 BC). Possibly re-created by J as his individualistic, stern, unbending, warlike 'stiff-necked' deity, with all his sensitive, jealous, demanding qualities. But there is no denying his close relationship with those early primitive gods of ancient sagas and folklore and of all neighbouring countries, with all their manlike emotions and irascibility, though supernatural, making onerous demands on their human subjects. Of such material was J's Yahweh fashioned. Hence his turbulent, ever-demanding, yet unfeeling, insensitive, remorseless, punishing nature. The major difference lay in the solid inflexibility of these graven images compared with the divine spirit of Yahweh.

The first Yahweh not only behaves like a capricious man (or even worse), but also makes mistakes and false promises (but rarely false threats); he never shows his face, but habitually makes forthright demands and blood-curdling threats. He regards Adam's family and descendants as imperfect and behaving so badly, that he makes his first awesome decision to destroy all his first Creation, and start again with the one good family of Noah, and a collection of specimens chosen from all animal life.

This is his second drastic action, after throwing Adam and Eve out of his specially created paradise of the garden of Eden and causing problems of intermarriage within the original family. But why plant the Tree of Life and Knowledge in the middle of Eden if he did not wish them to taste the fruit? The only answer is suggested by the Kabbala, the mystic book of the faith, which is built around the Tree of Life, with its crown reaching into heaven and its roots buried deep into the fertility of the earth, as will be discussed later.

103

Yahweh has to become militant, in order to strengthen and support his Israelites through all the battles of Canaan, to assist them to win through to his 'Promised Land'. Moses says: 'The Lord is a man of war'. (Exodus 15) Yahweh promises to 'destroy all the people to whom they shall come' (Exodus 23:27–30) He knows that they will have to beat them all by superior strategy and ferocity. It will take a long time before he can be transformed into the distant, invisible, quiet, gentle, merciful 'Father in Heaven' of the later part of the Bible, and allow the priests to 'take over the reins' after the Prophets have reshaped him in gentler form.

In the meantime he still delights in dealing out death in all forms. His second wholesale drowning is that of the Egyptians in the Red Sea. He slaughters whole nations and cities at a stroke. When the Israelites cavort with the daughters of Moab he orders Moses: 'Take all the heads of the people, and hang them up before the Lord against the Sun.' (Numbers 25:4) He dispenses heavy punishments. He will punish the very children for the sins of their fathers, their grandfathers, even their great-grandfathers. (Exodus 20:5-6) When they worship the Golden Calf at Sinai, he is so furious he again seeks to destroy them all – and Moses, despite his own anger, has to argue him out of it: 'Turn from thy fierce wrath and repent of the evil against thy people.' (Exodus 32:11–14) He is insensitive to their feelings, suffering and hardship, hunger and thirst. He is concerned only with his own needs and demands for sole worship and complete obedience, without any grumbling or backsliding. He knows no mercy, has no sympathy, simply punishes every slightest misdemeanour to the point of death or destruction. To be feared and obeyed, for there was no escape.

Yahweh again desires to exterminate them entirely for rebelling against Moses, and offers to start a new creation from

Moses himself – as ill-fated previously from Noah. But patient, wise Moses appeals to his better nature (which he has not yet shown) or his self-esteem, at what the rest of the world would think of such behaviour. An amusing scene of Moses holding a mirror up to Yahweh, to get a shock view of his future image to mankind, belittled by such contrary conduct. Moses was too wise to trust this new offer of Yahweh. What peace could he expect in founding his own nation? Another broken promise? More mass destruction from instant anger?

How could faithful old Abraham (now well over 100) accept his deity's diabolical command to sacrifice his only son Isaac (already over 30), on an altar to Yahweh? How could he go home to face the redoubtable Sarah? But Abraham gets his own back after passing this soul-searching test of Yahweh, who is so fond of imposing these severe, stringent challenges on his chosen champions, whom he never trusts implicitly, and has to keep checking and prodding. He teaches assertive Yahweh a lesson in moral ethics and judgement, by bargaining with him over his latest plan of total destruction of Sodom and Gomorrah.

The final passages of exhortation in Deuteronomy end with the most horrific curses imaginable on any who dare misbehave in the slightest, after all the Laws, Commandments and instructions on religious observances and those on food and hygiene and cleanliness, are given forth in minutest detail: 'Cursed shall be the fruit of thy body and the fruit of thy land... cursed shalt thou be when thou comest in ... and when thou goest out.... The Lord shall smite thee with madness, and blindness.... Also every sickness, and every plague, which is not written in the Book of the Law, them will the Lord bring upon thee, until thou be destroyed.' (Deuteronomy 28:16–28,61) Worse than excommunication! Prime example of the art of gentle persuasion!

However, Yahweh had to recognise the existence of other gods as, in his first Commandment, he demands that he be placed above them: 'Thou shalt have no other gods before me.' He orders his people to 'utterly overthrow his rivals' (Exodus 20:5,34) They had retained many other gods. Moses sings: 'Who is like unto thee, O Lord among the gods?' (Exodus 15:11) Solomon says: 'Great is our god above all other gods'. (2 Chronicles 2:5) Jeremiah accuses them: 'according to the number of thy cities are thy gods, O Judah,' protesting against their worship of Baal and Moloch. (Jeremiah 2:88,32:35)

Solomon's Temple finally committed the Jews to their worship of Yahweh as the One God, though it was based on fear rather than love. There was no hint of mercy or consideration to any sinner by Yaweh or the priests, nor any possibility of forgiveness. No wonder the people were reluctant to give up the graven images which brought them comfort, and did not blame, threaten or answer them back, or fill them with fear or dread. For example, the Ark of the Covenant, containing the sacred scrolls of the law, was untouchable. When pious Uzzah caught the Ark, to prevent it falling, 'The anger of the Lord was kindled against Uzzah, and God smote him there for his error, and there he died.' (2 Samuel 6:7). Today he would have been given a medal.

Sin was the all important main feature in Judiac theology. Virtue was its highest reward. Sin was inevitable and prevalent (the flesh was weak), with all its consequences from plague, disease and drought to defeat, or descent to Sheol, the 'shades of darkness' beneath the earth which received the dead, waiting in spiritual transparency. There was no immortality, life had to be completed with all its joys and sorrows. There was no other life after death. The only hope against sin was prayer or sacrifice, which began with humans, then animals and the best of the harvest – finally by offering praise and

106

devotion. Donations were eventually accepted by the priests as atonement for most sins, to be continued through the ages, satisfying both sides, for redemption. Now one tells one's beads, utters a few prayers or carries out some act of atonement.

The priests were a closed caste of the tribe Levi, supposedly without inheritance of property, but were exempt from tax. They levied a tithe upon the harvests and the flocks, and shared all offerings. The people were responsible for priestly dwellings, clothing and upkeep. Their wealth grew to give them almost as much power as the king. But they still could not stop the worship of the alien gods and the secret rites to Baal and Astarte, even by Solomon. Holy men like Elijah, Amos and Elisha preached against these practices and set a good example. Above all, the prophets who sought no personal gain, the supreme preachers, instructors and predictors, tried to guide the people to the true faith. The growing gap between the poor and wealthy, between city and country, prepared the way for the final disintegration of David's Kingdom into Israel in the north and Judah in the south and Jerusalem.

The Prophets (called Nabi) appeared. Amos left his sheep to visit Beth-el and was horrified by the life there, which he proclaimed against bitterly. Hosea said: 'They have sown the wind and shall reap the whirlwind.' (Hosea 8:6-7). Isaiah pleaded with King Ahaz and then King Hezekiah to stay neutral in the war between Assyria and Israel, foretelling its fateful end. But when King Sennacherib besieged Jerusalem, Isaiah counselled Hezekiah not to yield. He prophesied the downfall of Assyria, Moab, Syria, Ethiopia, Egypt and Babylon – but this was not fully confirmed. He accused the wealthy on behalf of Yahweh: 'Ye beat my people to pieces, and grind the faces of the poor.' But there came no intercession from Yahweh. The suffering of the people and the downtrodden did not seem to move him.

The Prophets were the best guides and influence for the people recovering from Babylonian exile, with their full support through difficult destitution. Amos and Isaiah changed Yahweh into a softer, gentler deity. The priests had to learn the real needs of the people from the prophets who lived closer to them, and were not selfishly power hungry and acquisitive like so many priests. They resolved to issue to the people a new, revised code of laws, to redress the moral life of the nation. King Josiah sought a religious revival, and priest Hilkiah 'found' a scroll of Moses amongst the ruins of the Temple. Josiah read the Book of the Covenant to the elders in the presence of thousands of people. He then smashed Baal and all the other idols and their altars and, following Jeremiah, he removed many greedy, self-seeking priests, proclaiming against their unworthiness and betrayal of their duties to the people.

Courageous little Judah fell subject first to Egypt, then to Babylon. Josiah was killed by an Egyptian arrow at Megiddo. Then Nebuchadnezzar beat Pharaoh Necho, and made Judah a Babylonian dependency. When they rose in revolt, seeking freedom, he captured Jerusalem, took King Jehoiakim prisoner, and put Zedekiah on the throne of Judah, taking 10,000 Jews into bondage. Zedekiah finally rebelled, so Nebuchadnezzar returned, burnt Jerusalem and destroyed the Temple. He killed Zedikiah's sons before his eyes, then blinded him and carried him and the rest of the population into captivity in Babylonia. There they sang Psalm 137:

'By the rivers of Babylon there we sat down,
Yea we wept when we remembered Zion ...
How shall we sing the Lord's song in a strange land?

108

If I forget thee, O Jerusalem, let my right hand forget her
cunning,
If I do not remember thee, let my tongue cleave to the roof
of my mouth;
If I set not Jerusalem above my chief joy.'

Jeremiah condemned Israel and the priests (who in revenge
sought his death), denounced the rulers of Judah as obstinate
fools, and advised complete surrender to Nebuchadnezzar,
King of Babylon. His book of prophesies is most eloquent,
passionate and sincere. He was completely honest and forthright, so feared by many: 'I have neither lent on usury, nor
men have lent to me on usury; yet every one of them doth
curse me.' (Jeremiah 15:10, 20:14) He called Israel to repentance saying Yahweh was punishing them for their sins,
iniquity and perversion: Men 'were as fed horses in the
morning; everyone neighed after his neighbour's wife'.
(Jeremiah 5:8) He denounced the priests as almost as false
and corrupt as the merchants. The priests tried to stop him
by putting his head in the stocks, but he continued to
denounce them. They sought to kill him, but Hilkiah's son
helped him escape. Finally he wrote his Lamentations, the
most eloquent book in the Old Testament, describing the
misery of the vanquished and desolate. 'They that are slain
with the sword are better than they that are slain with
hunger.' (Jeremiah 4:9)

Meanwhile in Babylon, Ezekiel began preaching with fierce
denunciations of idolatry and corruption in Jerusalem. He
made great lists of Jerusalem's sins, and then foretold her
capture and destruction but final resurrection. But the Israelites flourished in Babylon. Their freedom of movement and
worship, increased in numbers and wealth. Some followed the
customs and gods of Babylon. The new younger generations
almost forgot Jerusalem. But the pious renewed their Bible

and refreshed their religion, giving it new life, in preparation for their return to Jerusalem.

A 'second Isaiah' gave back the exiles their faith in monotheism, with a new Yahweh, in place of the old, fierce deity: 'The spirit of the Lord is upon me, because the Lord hath anointed me to bring good tidings unto the meek; He hath sent me to bind up the broken hearted, To proclaim liberty to the captives, and the opening of the prison to them that are bound.' (Isaiah 61:1)

He has had a revelation that Yahweh is not just a god of war and vengeance, but a loving Father who will rescue his people. He predicts that Persia will be the instrument of this libera-tion. Cyrus will take Babylon and free the Jews to return to rebuild Jerusalem, with a new temple. He proclaims: 'I am God, and there is none else; I am God, and there is none like Me.' (Ezekiel 46:9) He eloquently describes his Lord: 'who hath measured the waters in the hollow of his hand, and meted out heaven with the span, and comprehended the dust of the earth in a measure, and weighed the mountains in scales and the hills in a balance?... Behold, the nations are as a drop of a bucket ... All the nations are as nothing before Him; ... To whom, then will ye liken God? ... He maketh the judges of the earth as a thing of nought ... Lift up your eyes on high and see who hath created these.' (Ezekiel 40:12-26) Such beautiful poetic wording and phrasing. The Old Testa-ment is eloquent with so much lyrical poetry and prose, still not fully appreciated.

Cyrus took Babylon and returned their property, with the gold and silver taken from the Temple, and helped the returning exiles on their long homeward journey after 50 years. Cyrus sent Nehemiah, his chief of staff, with funds and an armed

110

escort to see to the rebuilding of Jerusalem and its fortifications. He sent for Ezra to support his efforts.

About 444 BC Ezra read to the people's assembly the Torah, Book of the Law of Moses, for seven days. Thereafter all swore to obey the Torah forever. (Nehemiah 10:29) Since then the Law has been the foundation stone of the life of the Jews, who have remained ever-loyal to it through the worst tortures, and vicissitudes, with unshakeable steadfastness to their faith. It became the bedrock of Christianity with the Ten Commandments and the Mosaic Laws, features also of Islam.

The Mosaic Code became the basis of future Jewish life, based on the books of Ezra and Josiah and the Ten Commandments. Religion underpinned statesmanship and encompassed every detail of life. It included all personal hygiene and conduct, and detailed cleanliness of food and diet. Their influence extended over the greater part of the world. King Minos was given the laws to govern Crete; the Greeks had Dionysus called the Lawgiver, with two tablets of stone on which laws were inscribed, and Zoroaster had 'The Book of the Law' delivered by Ahura-Mazda.

The Old Testament combines history, drama, religion and laws, wars and feuds, with romance, poetry and philosophy in profusion. The stories of Moses, David and Solomon have no match in quality and style and richness of colourful content. Genesis, however we stress its myth-like quality, is a powerful epic, told plainly and simply with its colourful panorama of the Creation and all its consequences. It is the outstanding effort of J, the unknown, original and greatest biblical author, to weave the ancient myths, epics and folk legends into the ancient history of his own people. To gather countless years of previous ancient history in a most attractive form. He develops his own style and narrative ability as the most gifted

111

writer of the whole Bible. Truly there is none to compare with him, for his was the creation which has come down through the ages, still exists, and has outlasted all others, as the foundation of the Eastern and Western religions.

Biblical Romances abound: Abraham and his doughty Sarah, Isaac and Rebecca, Jacob and Rachel, Samson and Delilah, Esther, Judith and Daniel. Poetry of the highest quality (the song of Moses (Exodus 15), song of Deborah (Judges 5)), permeates the Pentateuch, especially David's outpourings in the Psalms and the longing for home as in the Babylonian exile, and echo through the centuries in the works of many great authors. The Psalms, above all, are generally accepted as the world's finest lyrical expressions, enhanced by the wisdom of the Proverbs. They are a complete poetical mixture of tenderness and humility. 'As for man, his days are as grass; as a flower of the field, so he flourisheth. For the wind passes over it, and it is gone, and the place thereof shall know it no more.' (Psalms 103:15–16) Heroic valour to humble pleas, fine imagery with metaphor and similes and above all, a deeply held religious faith.

The Song of Solomon differs, however, with its abundance of joyful lyrics of freely expressed romance, from the more contained language of the Old Testament: 'There be three things which are wonderful to me, yea four which I know not: the way of an eagle in the air, the way of a serpent on a rock, the way of a ship in the midst of the sea, and the way of a man with a maid.' (Proverbs 30:18–19) 'Work is wisdom, words are mere folly.' 'In all labour there is profit, but the talk of the lips tendeth only to penury ... A fool uttereth all his mind, but a wise man keepeth it in till afterwards... even a fool, when he holdeth his peace, is counted wise.' (Proverbs 14:23,17:28) 'Happy is the man that findeth wisdom and the man that getteth understanding.... She is more precious than rubies.…. Her ways are ways of pleasantness, and all her paths are peace.' (Proverbs 16:23.3:13-17) 'He that giveth to the poor, shall not lack.' (Proverbs 28:27) 'A man's pride shall bring him low; but he that is of lowly spirit shall obtain honour.' (Proverbs 29:23) 'An unjust man is an abomination to the righteous.' (Proverbs 29:27) There is so much wisdom in the Old 'Original' Testament that solutions may be found for most of the problems of this world and mankind. Only Ecclesiastes, the preacher son of David, casts doubt on the whole panorama of religion. His scepticism dismantles much of the carefully built structure, developed with such zeal by differing contributors, destroying the hopes and optimism of life in its fullness 'while the evil days come not', with hope reduced to despair. It is the warning not to take everything written and propounded at its face value. Despite its fascinating arc of brilliant colours, there is no crock of gold at the base of every rainbow. Do not be deceived by the outer shell.

Jerusalem rises again, first as a vassal city to Persia, then of Greece. In 334 BC Alexander, before his untimely death, admired and wished to rebuild Jerusalem, but finally came the destruction by the Romans and total Exile. Through it all Jerusalem has continued to rise and fall and rise again, as of now. Always she has built a race of heroes from her founder, the great King David, to the world-famous epic of the Six-Day War. Now once again and, we trust, finally, Jerusalem is the centre of brave Israel, this time to rebuild and hold supremely, with the sincere admiration of the world. Deservedly so, for after all it was the Jews who first brought history, civilisation and a lasting religious faith to the world. Now it must seek to bring lasting peace as its present supreme mission, first with its neighbours, the Arabs, who share the same Semitic roots, then with all other countries, especially those who cry aloud for relief from their suffering, to whom we all owe equal duty.

113

5

LEVITICUS

Leviticus, the Book of the Priests, is an exhaustive and exhausting category of every conceivable duty and reward for the priests. Not only priestly duties but also all regular payments of tithes, sacrifices, best fruits of the harvest, all care and attention due to them, with even land set aside with housing and without cost as they were not supposed to own property, and no menial tasks. They cannot be expected to partake of the men's normal labours or battles... their duty is to minister at the Tabernacles, the Tent of the Meeting, and lead them all in prayers and pleas. Chapter 16 quotes further benefits for the priests, itemising their very special holy garments, including pure linen tunics, linen breeches with a linen girdle and a linen mitre. Evidently the priests were most concerned with themselves and enhancing their powerful position, with all the care to be taken of them by the people, and details of food, clothing, gifts and welfare to be supplied them in abundance. So much so, that instead of detailing the services they owed the people, they were busily listing all the duties of the people to them.

'Whatsoever parteth the hoof and is wholly cloven-footed, and cheweth the cud among the beasts, that may ye eat. Nevertheless these shall ye not eat, of them that only chew the cud, or of them that only part the hoof; the camel... rock-badger... the hare and swine... they are unclean to you.' (Leviticus 11. 3–8)

'This is the law of the beast, and of the fowl and every living creature that moveth in the waters... and swarmeth upon the earth; to make a difference between the clean and unclean.' (Leviticus 11: 16–17)

This is an itemised list of what may be eaten and what is 'unclean' and therefore unfit to be eaten. Followed by all the treatments from birth to death, including circumcision at eight days old, and all the sickness, diseases and infirmities itemised with their treatments. All vitally necessary in their continuous battle against both elements and enemies, and already laid down by Moses.

Especial interest in diseases, with major attention to the plague. Of amusing interest to modern man is Leviticus 13:40-45: 'And if a man's hair be fallen off his head, he is bald, yet is he clean. And if his hair be fallen off from the front part of his head, he is forehead bald; yet is he clean. But if there be in the bald head, or the bald forehead a reddish-white plague, it is leprosy breaking out in his bald-head, or his bald forehead'... 'And the leper in whom the plague is, his clothes shall be rent, and the hair of his head go loose, and he shall cover his upper lips and shall cry: "Unclean, unclean."' If and when he is cured, further detailed directions follow: 'And it shall be on the seventh day that he shall shave all his hair off his head, and his beard and his eyebrows, even all his hair shall he shave off.' (Leviticus 14:9)

Leviticus also warns the people concerning their conduct and proper worship of Yahweh, not only now but later in Canaan: 'I am the Lord your God. After the doings of the land of Egypt... shall ye not do; and after the doings of the land of Canaan... shall ye not do.... Ye shall therefore keep my ordinances.' (Leviticus 18:2–5) We hear the voice of the priests seeking already to assume their sought-after rôle, as

115

interpreters of Yahweh's commands to the people, and acting as his voice in their desire to assume full power *in loco parentis*. Here, due warning is given from Yahweh, the 'Jealous God', of what to expect should they wander off to their old gods in Egypt, or worship the new gods they will encounter in Canaan. But of course his 'stiff-necked people' soon broke all his ordinances and took to Baal and Astarte with a will, as also enjoying the delights of the daughters of Moab.

'Turn ye not unto the ghosts, nor unto familiar spirits.' (Leviticus 19:22) Even Saul could not resist calling up Samuel's spirit to seek his advice. Then sage advice given to 'honour the face of the old man' and 'the stranger that sojourneth with you shall be unto you as the home-born among you, and thou shalt love him as thyself; for ye were strangers in the land of Egypt.' (Leviticus 19:31-34) (But failed to add 'and look what they did to you'.) 'And if a man lie with mankind, as with womankind, both of them have committed abomination.' (Leviticus 20:13) 'A man or a woman that divineth by a ghost, or a familiar spirit, shall surely be put to death.' (Leviticus 20:27)

Chapter 23 details the holy Convocations, especially 'Six days shall work be done; but on the seventh day is a Sabbath of Solemn rest... ye shall do no manner of work.' (Leviticus 23:3) 'Six years thou shalt sow thy field.... But in the seventh year shall be a Sabbath of solemn rest for the land... thou shalt neither sow thy field, nor prune thy vineyard.' (Leviticus 25:34) 'A jubilee shall that fiftieth year be unto you; ye shall not sew, neither reap that which groweth of itself in it, nor gather the grapes of the undressed vines.' (Leviticus 25:11) 'And if a man sell a dwelling-house in a walled city, then he may redeem it within a whole year after it is sold; for a full year shall he have the right of redemption.' (Leviticus 25:29)

116

It is truly amazing to look back on those ancient times and picture this development gradually evolving. From a downtrodden people in forced slavery of lowest level, to a homogenous, rapidly increasing whole nation, under a truly great leader, midst all their wars and battles and inner strife and struggles for life, and note the fine detail covering every possible circumstance. Surely records must have been kept to the knowledge of these writers. How much time and thought must have been devoted with deep meditation to produce such a wide variety of measures for their protection, in every possible detail and circumstance. The few examples quoted of especial interest to us serve to show their complete coverage of all facets of life to protect their people. These were not idle people in any way, nor did they lack for spiritual as well as wordly guidance. Above all must their leader Moses have been a truly great and wise, far-seeing man, a hero of great stature, yet overall quiet, modest, patient and caring for his people's every need. Such great leaders arise but once in a millennium, and are rarely accorded their full recognition or honour till long after their death.

'Ye shall make you no idols.' (Leviticus 26:1) Such warnings are followed by the blessings to be received by those keeping the Commandments (an enormous task to keep them all), and the dire punishments to be expected for disobedience: 'And yet for all that, when they are in the land of their enemies, I will not reject them, neither will I abhor them, to destroy them utterly, and to break my covenant with them; for I am the Lord their God.' (Leviticus 26:44)

Yet in all truth Yahweh did break his covenants, repeatedly, and permitted torture, death and slaughter in mass numbers of his 'chosen people'. Harsh treatment which outdid all those heavy sentences of J's Yahweh (for whose portrayal many have since condemned J) meted out to his first Creation of

117

mankind, through thousands of years leading up to the final Holocaust of the Nazi Germans, well supported by Austria, France, Belgium, Hungary, Holland, Poland and Russia with the assent of their Governments and the Roman Catholic church. One wonders whether all these covenants and promises may now be made good, finally with the world and church's genuine apologies, with the rebirth of that small fragment of Israel's original 'Promised Land' and David's hard-won Kingdom. Even now insufficient effort is being made by the world, with the great exception of the outstanding honourable efforts of America, to ensure that this recovered, tiny State of Israel, be left in peace to work for its own good and for the benefits they can bring the rest of the world.

Leviticus is understood to have been largely the product of P's priestly group, still striving to firm up their position of power and significance in the hierarchy, and take credit for Moses' great work. We do not know what part Aaron may have played in the production of all those detailed ordinances. It is of such tremendous scope and such detailed analysis that it would seem impossible to have been encompassed by one man alone. J the originator must have set the scene, and devoted much time of research and thought to the huge breadth of the work he undertook. But we have no indication nor clues as yet to what contributions his successors made. They cannot just be summarised under E, D or P, even R as the final Redactor who put all their efforts and versions together. Well-known scribes, writers, prophets and priests, as well as kings, from David to Josiah, with other leading figures, to name only Zadok, Adonijah and Hilkiah, Ezra and Jeremiah (who may have produced Deuteronomy's two versions) – will all have contributed their part. Also the great figures of the Prophets who added the wisdom of their books. Records must still somehow, somewhere exist, to give factual credence to all these tales and ordinances, similar to the scrolls discovered in the caves.

Yet there remain many as yet unknown, unmentioned characters who may well have made their own contributions to all that kaleidoscope of myriad scenes which make up the Bible, still the greatest book in the world, in what is familiarly known as the Old Testament – or better still, for me, the Original Testament.

6

NUMBERS

The tribes of Israel were chosen by Moses from the 12 sons of Jacob, whose name was changed to Israel. They became the 'Princes of Israel'. From them came the divisions of troops with their appointed leaders. 'All that were able to go forth to war... numbered 603,550.' How could they make such exact calculations without written records, of which, mysteriously, none have been found? The discovery of the Dead Sea Scrolls gives hope that ancient records may still survive, maybe for our archaeologists and geologists to unearth. 'But the Levites, after the tribe of their fathers, were not numbered among them.' (Numbers 1:45-47) The Levites, Moses' own tribe, were assigned by him to be priests to attend the Tabernacle and carry out all the priestly duties, instead of fighting. It did not take them long to attain the full power and benefits of such position, until they were accepted as Yahweh's voice and interpreter and future guides in moral virtues, prayer, sacrifice, conduct and good behaviour.

Moses, as leader, arranged his plans of division under appointed tribal and army leaders, with each apportioned his duties. His was the tremendous task of trying to keep that difficult, self-opinionated, unruly mass of recently released slaves in good shape and order. The work of marshalling them into composite groups must have been daunting from the very outset. No records have been discovered as yet, but they must have existed; with tallies, accounts, plans and designs, as well as some written history of the adventures and development of this great multitude which grew to over 2 million souls – either numbered by Moses or Aaron or their scribes.

Yet of all the scrolls and tablets unearthed in their many thousands from the palaces, museums, libraries of other neighbouring countries, not a single record has so far been found of these great events. Are we then to assume that Moses kept no records, though it is clearly stated that Yahweh instructed him to write down His Commandments, to be passed on to his Children of Israel? To assume it all to have sprung from J alone, is to conceive of the most stupendous creative story writing by J, making him the most outstanding author of the whole world. Even Shakespeare sought his material elsewhere, turning to Coverdale's Geneva Bible for much of his inspiration. The detailed composition of Numbers alone, with those never-ending 'begats', could have amounted to one scribe's life work of chronology. Much is repeated in Leviticus and again in Deuteronomy, suggesting the work of many scribes and writers, well-known to J and other authors. It would have been well-nigh impossible to remember them by rote and pass them on orally, correct in every detail.

Chapter 4 details the 'service of the sons of Kohath in the Tent of Meeting', and the duties of the sons of Gershon (was he the son of Moses?) within the Tent of the Meeting, all scrupulously categorised 'at the command of Aaron and his sons', as also the sons of Merari. So they were quite a consortium attending to all details inside and outside the Tent of the Meeting under the priests.

Chapter 5 excludes all lepers from the camp and 'whosoever is unclean by the dead'. Then deals with all family and marital problems, detailing tests of constancy. Followed by the mode of conduct of men and women who desire to consecrate themselves to the service of the Lord 'the vow of the Nazirite'. 'And the Nazirite shall shave the head of his separation – and put it (his hair) on the fire which is under the sacrifice of peace offerings.' (Hence the later monk's tonsure).

Yahweh now lays down for Aaron and sons the form of blessing of the people, still preserved in exact wording:

'The Lord bless thee, and keep thee;
The Lord make his face to shine upon thee, and give thee peace.' (Numbers 6:24-26)

'And the princes offered for the dedication of the altar... their oblation before the altar' and very bountiful were their offerings. The details of all these tremendous offerings fill chapters 6-8, finishing with the length of service of the Levites from age 25 until 50 years: 'and shall serve no more'. (Numbers 8:24-26) No mention of a pension at 50. What would they do – live off their tithes and offerings? They soon devised other means to become wealthy and powerful, obviously occupying higher positions in later years. Thus do little empires grow – and still continue, always adaptable to all bureaucratic circumstances.

However, this 'stiff-necked' (obstinate) people cannot remain long without grumbling and groaning. 'And the mixed multitude... fell a lusting: and the Children of Israel also wept again and said, Who shall give us flesh to eat?' 'We remember the fish which we did eat in Egypt for nought.' 'We have nought save this manna to look to ... . and the anger of the Lord was kindled greatly.' (Numbers 11:4–6) Yahweh's answer: 'Ye shall not eat (meat) one day, nor two days, nor five days, neither ten days, nor twenty days. But a whole month, until it come out at your nostrils, and it be loathsome unto you.' (Numbers 11:19-20) But instead of carrying out his threat, having sent them a swarm of quails which they gathered day and night. 'While the flesh was yet between their teeth, ere it was chewed, the anger of the Lord was kindled against the people and the Lord smote the people with a very great *plague* (another use of his favourite weapon). And the name of that place was called Kibroth-Lattaavah; because that they buried the people that lusted.' (Numbers 11:33-34).

So once more Yahweh broke his word, because he again lost his temper. Not satisfied with making them eat quail flesh until they sickened of it – an unduly harsh, unfeeling punishment for requesting a change from the everlasting manna – Yahweh burns with anger, and sends them a deadly plague to kill them as they ate. Modern parlance would call that 'over the top'. It was not a criminal action by the people.

J now gives us a well-earned interlude from Yahweh's deadly, harsh punishments. In Chapter 12 we are treated to some local gossip. Miriam and Aaron, maybe jealous of Moses' top position as leader and lawgiver, indulge in some unpleasant gossip about the Cushite woman they claimed Moses had married – a Cushite which some called a dark Egyptian. Miriam was sister both to Moses and Aaron – but she is jealous of Moses' highest standing: 'And they said, Hath the Lord indeed spoken only with Moses? Hath he not spoken only with us? And the Lord heard it' (Numbers 12:2) (listening to gossip?). Moses is now described as 'very meek, above all the men which were upon the face of the earth'. So he does not defend himself. Instead Yahweh's anger was 'kindled against them' and he turned Miriam 'leprous, as white as snow'. Aaron pleads to Moses and good Moses pleads to Yahweh for his sister, well-known as Miriam the Prophetess. 'And the Lord said unto Moses, If her father had but spit in her face should she not be ashamed seven days?' (Numbers 12:14) So Yahweh ordered Miriam to be shut outside the camp for seven days until cured. A neat tale as entr'acte between two tragedies.

Chapter 13 returns us to more serious matters: Yahweh orders Moses to send men to 'spy out the land of Canaan, which I give unto the children of Israel' (who turn out to be more like the grandchildren). Twelve men with Joshua. They brought back grapes, pomegranates and figs, after 40 days, saying: 'it floweth with milk and honey'. But they claimed they saw 'men of great stature' 'and we were in our own sight as grasshoppers'. So the people are scared, despite reassurance from Joshua and Caleb. Frightened, they want to run all the way back to Egypt. Now they have truly roused the wrath of Yahweh. 'And the Lord said unto Moses: How long will this people despise me? and how long will they not believe in me? I will smite them with the pestilence, and disinherit them, and will make of *thee* a nation greater and mightier than they.' (Numbers 14:11-12)

But wise Moses has the diplomatic answer: 'Then the Egyptians shall hear it... and they will tell it to the inhabitants of this land; they have heard that thou Lord art in the midst of this people... then the nations which have heard the fame of thee, will speak saying, Because the Lord was not able to bring this people into the land which he sware unto them, therefore he hath slain them in the wilderness.' (Numbers 14:13-16) Moses persuades as follows, supplying Yahweh with his escape clause, cunningly suggesting: 'The Lord is slow to anger and plenteous in mercy (ouch!), forgiving iniquity and transgression, and that will by no means clear the guilty; visiting the iniquity of the fathers upon the children, upon the third and upon the fourth generation.' (Numbers 14:18-19)

Moses has won the argument, but at what terrible cost. Yahweh sees the point but counters with a devastating death

124

blow; unforgiving of 'all those men which have seen my glory, and my signs, which I wrought in Egypt and in the wilderness, yet have tempted me these ten times, and have not hearkened to my voice: Surely they shall not see the land which I sware unto their fathers.' 'How long shall I bear with this evil congregation.... Say unto them, As I live, saith the Lord.... Your carcases shall fall in this wilderness... from *twenty years old* and upward.... But your little ones... them will I bring in.' (Numbers 14:22–31). 'And your children shall be wanderers in the wilderness forty years.' (Numbers 14:33). He even sent the Amalekites and Canaanites down to smite them. Imagine their feelings at such unjust, unmerciful sentence of death – even to deprive the children of their parents!

Yet in the very next chapter Yahweh goes into complete details, ordering exactly what sacrifices must be prepared and made for him. He condemns a man gathering sticks on the Sabbath day to death by stoning. Then makes holy orders regarding fringes on their garments to remind them of Yahweh's commandments. He veers from one extreme to the other. Having just condemned them to death, he now gives detailed instructions on their manner of worship of him, and keeping his Commandments. It is like visiting the condemned prisoner in his cell and giving him detailed instructions on obeying the Commandments and saying his prayers in worship of the one who has condemned him to death. How insensitive and extremist.

The terrible condemnation to death of all those over 20 years old, now switches to the more minor episode of the attempted revolt in Chapter 16, against Moses and Aaron, by Korah of their own tribe of Levi, supported by Dathan and Abiram and 250 princes and other men. They reproached Moses and Aaron, saying: 'Ye take too much upon you, seeing all the congregation are holy... wherefore then lift ye up yourselves

125

above the assembly of the Lord?' (Numbers 16: 1–3) (echoes of modern priestly power struggles). Drastic punishment followed from Yahweh: 'And the earth opened her mouth and swallowed them up, and their households.' (Numbers 16:32)

But the Israelites still had not learnt from this sharp lesson: 'but on the morrow, all the congregation of the children of Israel murmured against Moses, and against Aaron, saying: Ye have killed the people of the Lord.' (Numbers 16:41) 'And the Lord spake unto Moses, saying, Get you up from among this congregation that I may consume them in a moment.' (Numbers 16:45) The plague began immediately, before Moses had time to make his usual intercession, standing bravely 'between the dead and the living', and the plague was stayed. 'Now they that died by the plague were fourteen thousand and seven hundred, beside them that died about the matter of Korah'. (Numbers 16:48-49). It is truly amazing that this 'stiff-necked people' were not completely cowed by such devastating punishment, and wholesale murder at any deviation, grumble, strike or semi-revolt.

Yahweh then devised a more peaceful end to the attempted revolt against Moses' leadership. Each of the 12 princes of the 12 tribes was given a rod with his name printed. Aaron's rod for the house of Levi 'was budded, and put forth buds, and bloomed blossoms, and bore ripe almonds'. (Numbers 17:8) 'And the children of Israel spake unto Moses, saying, Behold, we perish, we are undone, we are all undone.' (Numbers 17:12) In other words 'the fear of the Lord is the beginning of wisdom'. It is a strong feature of J's creative talent that he is able to paint a major scene in a few stark strokes.

Moses' next problem came in the wilderness of Zin, with lack of water. 'And the people strove with Moses and spake, saying: Would God that we had died when our brethren died

126

before the Lord!' (Numbers 20:3) Then followed the episode of Moses striking the rock, at Yahweh's behest, to produce water. But Yahweh, once more most jealous and displeased at not being lauded and praised for his beneficence, now blames Moses and Aaron: 'Because ye believed not in me, to *sanctify* me in the eyes of the children of Israel, therefore ye shall not bring this assembly into the land which I have given them.' (Numbers 20:12) Was there ever a harsher, more unjust, sentence passed upon a truly great leader, who had almost daily to quieten the mob for some grumble or complaint or attempted revolt, and at the same time intercede on their behalf with Yahweh, who was subject to fierce anger easily provoked, meting out harsh punishments including death. When he cannot kick the awkward Children of Israel, he takes his anger out unfairly on his meek, modest, patient, wise, chosen leader, almost like a spoilt child.

Control of a body of men, over time, is never an easy matter, and a good leader must be ever watchful and alert for the first signs of trouble, in order to be able to quell it before any heat grows. But to have at the same time to deal with a nervous, fractious, temperamental commander, known for immediate, over-hasty, fierce judgements and harsh punishments, makes matters far worse. J had the ability to portray the frailties of both sides. Here he plays upon our heart-strings, at Yahweh's terrible condemning to death both Moses and Aaron, denying them the long-promised entry into the Promised Land. No wonder later, priestly writers sought to soften J's unattractive portrayal of Yahweh, and even to remove the very name and change it for Adonai – the Lord, a God of quite different make-up in many ways. Yet even they could not rid their versions completely of all the strong, fearful characteristics of J's original Yahweh.

Aaron soon dies at Edom 'because ye rebelled against my

127

word at the waters of Menbah', and his son Eleazar is appointed in his place by Yahweh. The long journey continues with battles against the King of Arad in the South 'and they utterly destroyed them and their cities'. (Numbers 21:3) It must have been quite a relief to have something tangible to fight against. But they grew tired of these long, everlasting nomadic journeyings, and complained of no bread and no water 'and our soul loatheth this light bread' – the everlasting, unchangeable manna. So Yahweh sends them fiery serpents to bite and kill many of them. Then follows the story of the serpent of brass set on a standard, which cured their snake bites. A lighter touch to bring them to the well at Beer, and prepare them for further successful battles against the Amorites, and then Og the King of Bashan.

Now follows the amusing tale of Balak, King of Moab 'beyond the Jordan at Jericho', who was 'sore afraid of the people, because they were many.' (Numbers 22:3) So he sent for Balaam of Pethor, diviner, to come and curse the Israelites for Moab and Midian. Yahweh forbade Balaam at first, but later allowed him to go, but only to speak words given him by Yahweh. So Balaam saddles his faithful ass, and sets off with the princes of Moab. Then Yahweb changes his mind again and decides to play tricks on Balaam, just as he did at Babel, in mischievous fashion, sending an angel to block the way. 'And the ass saw the angel of the Lord standing in the way, with his sword drawn in his hand; and the ass turned aside out of the way, and went into the field; and Balaam smote the ass, to turn her into the way.' (Numbers 22:23) Again the angel appeared and the ass moved against the wall, crushing Balaam's foot, to be beaten again. The angel appeared a third time, and the ass lay down under Balaam, who smote her again.

The ass now speaks, to complain to Balaam: 'Was I ever wont

to do so unto thee? And he said: Nay. Then the Lord opened the eyes of Balaam, and he saw the angel of the Lord standing in the way, with his sword drawn in his hand; and he bowed his head, and fell on his face.' (Numbers 22:30–31) The angel explained why he had come, and that the ass had saved Balaam's life, so he had better do as now ordered by Yahweh: 'Go with the men; but only the word that I shall speak unto thee, that thou shalt speak.' (Numbers 22:35) So Balaam spoke as commanded: 'How shall I curse, whom God hath not cursed?.... And Balak said unto Balaam, What hast thou done unto me? I took thee to curse mine enemies, and, behold, thou hast blessed them altogether.'

So Balaam had fresh altars built, but spoke as Yahweh 'put a word in his mouth', saying: 'God is not a man, that he should lie; neither the son of man, that he should repent.' 'Behold I have received commandment to bless; and he hath blessed, and I cannot reverse it.' So Balak takes him to another place to try again. But Balaam produced the famous words: 'How goodly are thy tents, O Jacob, thy tabernacles, O Israel! As valleys are they spread forth, as gardens by the river side.... God bringeth him forth out of Egypt; he hath, as it were, the strength of the wild-ox; he shall eat up the nations his adversaries, and shall break their bones in pieces, and smite them through with his arrows.... Blessed be every one that blesseth thee; and cursed be every one that curseth thee... there shall come forth a star out of Jacob, and a sceptre shall arise out of Israel, and shall smite through the corners of Moab.' 'Alas, who shall live when God doeth this?' (Numbers chapters 22 to 24).

The result however, was that the Israelites dwelt peacefully in Moab: 'And Israel abode in Shittim, and the people began to commit whoredom with the daughters of Moab.... And Israel joined himself unto Baal-peor; and the anger of the Lord was kindled against Israel.' And the Lord said unto Moses: 'Take

129

all the chiefs of the people, and hang them up unto the Lord before the sun... and Moses said unto the judges of Israel, Slay ye every one his men that have joined themselves unto Baal-peor.' However, the day was saved by the action of Phinehas, son of Eleazar the priest, who saw a man with a Midianitish woman, in the sight of Moses... and all the congregation.' So he thrust a spear through them both 'and the plague was stayed from the children of Israel.' (Numbers 25:1–8) But 24,000 died of the plague in another fierce punishment by Yahweh, at the same time ordering Moses to smite the Midianites: 'For they vex you with their wiles, wherewith they have beguiled you in the matter of Peor.' (Numbers 25:18) False gods were not permitted.

Of interest for modern times is Chapter 27:8–11: 'If a man die and have no son, then ye shall cause his inheritance to pass unto his daughter. And if he have no daughter, then ye shall give his inheritance unto his brethren. And if he have no brethren, then ye shall give his inheritance unto his father's brethren. And if his father have no brethren, then ye shall give his inheritance unto his kinsman, that is next to him of his family.'

Then Yahweh spells out his doom once more to Moses: 'Get thee up into this mountain of Abarim, and behold the land which I have given unto the children of Israel. And when thou hast seen it, thou also shall be gathered unto thy people. Because ye rebelled against my word in the wilderness of Zin.' (Numbers 27:12-14) What a terrible fate to mete out to his most loyal, patient, long-suffering servant – and for no real crime. A final blow to the prestige of J's Yahweh. No wonder those who followed felt it incumbent upon them to change that bloodthirsty, intolerant, unforgiving image, before possible repudiation by his 'stiff-necked people' in favour of some more tolerant, amicable and forgiving deity.

130

Moses not only meekly accepts Yahweh's death sentence, but even suggests the appointment of his successor, Joshua, duly handing over command in good order. But Yahweh is not yet finished with his demands on his faithful servant. He now instructs him on the sacrifices and burnt-offerings and feast days with all the details to be passed on to his people. So Moses obeys and passes on full instructions, including the making of vows. Finally Yahweh demands: 'Avenge the children of Israel of the Midianites: afterward shalt thou be gathered unto thy people... and they warred against Midian... and slew every male.' So Moses had to serve and even fight a last battle before being relieved of his command.

However, some of the people were not so keen for entry into Canaan. The tribes of Reuben and Gad had much cattle and found the area of the land of Gilead most favourable for their use. So they asked Moses to be allowed to remain there and not go over Jordan into Canaan. Permission was granted on agreement to join in the battles to come until final victory. Then they would return to their chosen land. Chapter 33:2 records that 'Moses wrote their goings out according to their journeys by the commandment of the Lord.' But no records have ever been found of all their journeys. Aaron died in Mount Hor in their fortieth year after leaving Egypt. He was 123 years old.

Now follows a list of all their journeyings since leaving Egypt, and the division of the Promised Land according to the tribes, their size and worthiness. Also: 'Command that they give unto the Levites of the inheritance of their possession, cities to dwell in; and their suburbs shall be for their cattle... and the cities which ye shall give unto the Levites they shall be the six cities of refuge, which ye shall give for the manslayer to flee thither' (the first mention of places of refuge and safe haven). 'All the cities which ye shall give the Levites shall be forty and

131

eight cities.' (Numbers 35:2–7) 'Then ye shall appoint you cities to be cities of refuge for you; that the manslayer which killeth any person unwittingly may flee thither. And the cities shall be unto you for refuge from the avenger, that the manslayer die not until he stand before the congregation for judgement.' (Numbers 35:11) Then follows a list of possible judgements and family inheritance details, to close their wanderings, until finally reaching Canaan, to be entered by their children.

Numbers is a book which does not reflect well upon the behaviour of J's Yahweh. The only real hero to emerge head and shoulders above all others is Moses, their greatest leader, of infinite wisdom, modesty and patience. It contains some of the worst horror stories of J's conception, lightened only by the relief of cleverly interposed passages of J's ironic humour.

This was really J's final effort. His main great theme was above all Genesis, his greatest work, to which he obviously devoted deep research into all primitive ancestors. He was much influenced by the written records of the Sumerians, Assyrians, Babylonians, Persians and Egyptians and all their myths, stories and epics, especially their manlike, tough gods of similar nature to Yahweh.

Exodus was his classic Epic featuring the breathtaking escape of the Hebrews from hundreds of years of brutal bondage and final slavery under cruel Pharaohs. Followed by 40 long years of suffering, hardening, reshaping and discipline in the desolate great Wilderness of Zin, until they reached at last the entrance to that so often Promised Land. Only to be refused on the last lap and doomed to die there, with Moses their great leader, is starkest, almost unbearable tragedy – a scene worthy of Shakespeare at his most tragic. Leaving us dismayed and rebellious against J's Yahweh, who could perpetrate such destruction once again, of his own creatures. A terrible example of impossible celestial inhumanity, which could not be accepted or countenanced by future generations.

7

DEUTERONOMY

There is much controversy over the production of Deuteronomy, but the general agreement is that it was written by D, another unknown author, c 650 BC. There is even the suggestion that there may have been two editions of Deuteronomy, and that Hilkiah or more likely Jeremiah may have been the author. I believe there is another possibility. J, the original author, had his work, which was originally all in one continuous book, broken up by the Redactor into the three books of Genesis, Exodus and Numbers. Leviticus is obviously an extension of J by the P or priestly group of Aaronite priests, anxious to make their position, power and dues from the people abundantly clear. But Deuteronomy is a continuation and finalisation of Exodus, and obviously, with its similarity in style and context, originally the final part of J's version. J was so careful and exact in all his definitions that the main subject matter of Deuteronomy, the full text of Moses' final speech and his leave-taking of his people, must surely have been included by J to round off his great character.

Then along comes D, about 300 years later, keen to contribute to J's great work, who decides on an extended version of Moses' farewell to the Children of Israel. In fact the end of Numbers is somewhat artificially abrupt, and Deuteronomy would be a fitting close to Moses' wonderful leadership if it were a continuation of Numbers. Hence my belief that it was originally the final part of J's portrayal of Moses and his relationship with both Yahweh and the Children of Israel. It bears the hallmark of J's authorship. Finally it may have been the decision of the Redactor, 100 years later, to split J's work into five books, thus using Deuteronomy to round off his own first version of the early Bible.

We had in Numbers the details of Aaron's death in the fortieth year of their wanderings after Egypt. Now we have the demise of Moses soon after. There is obvious correlation, and little time left. So Moses makes his farewell speech 'beyond the Jordan, in the land of Moab', and addresses them: 'Behold I have set the land before you; go in and possess the land. Ye are this day as the stars of heaven for multitude.' (Deuteronomy 1:8 &10). He had trained them in peace and war, parents and children, and appointed wise men as heads, 'captains of thousands, and captains of hundreds... fifties and tens, and officers'. But then follows a repetition of past events, journeys, happenings, battles, disobedience, punishments – all culled from Exodus and Numbers, especially re-telling the tales of woe.

Now he must leave them at the point of entry into the Promised Land, in the hands of Joshua, his successor. Moses besought the Lord at that time saying: 'Let me go over, I pray thee, and see the good land that is beyond Jordan – and Lebanon. But the Lord was wroth with me for your sakes and hearkened not unto me.' (Deuteronomy 3:25-26) 'And now, O Israel, hearken unto the statutes, and unto the judgements, which I teach you, for to do them.' (Deuteronomy 4:1). D, for no valid reason, replaces J's Mount Sinai with Horeb, which is near but not as mountainous, and warns against making graven images. Moses warns them that if they 'deal corruptly, and make a graven image – and shall do that which is evil in the sight of the Lord thy God to provoke Him... ye shall soon utterly perish from off the land whereunto ye go over

135

Jordan to possess it.... And the Lord shall scatter you among the peoples.' (Deuteronomy 4:25–28) As always, these threats of dire punishment for disobedience, including death for worship of graven images, bear the stamp of dictatorship. Perhaps Moses was warning them in personal tones: 'Look what has happened to me – and I was guilty of no personal sins, but simply acted on your behalf to ease your problems of thirst and hunger.' Truly a merciless Yahweh is again presented by D (continuing J), hard, tough, unyielding, pitiless in meting out extreme punishments. These are heartfelt warnings by Moses as one who knows.

Each of the Ten Commandments is carefully explained, though they are basically simple and clear to all. But, as always, prefaced with: 'Thou shalt have no other gods before me.' Much controversy has followed, leading to the belief that Yahweh had to accept the reality of the situation that, come what may, they still would keep their other gods, as long as they acknowledged Yahweh as Supremo. Clearly Yahweh saw his strongest competition coming from those outstanding gods, Baal and Astarte, worshipped by all other peoples, enticing his Children of Israel to join them. Which they willingly continued to do, including their kings and leaders, judges and some priests, despite all the threats and punishments. J certainly understood the drawing power of such dumb images, which did not threaten nor punish, but rendered peaceful comfort by their very presence. Just as they still continue to do even now in many households.

Moses' clarion call is 'Hear, O Israel: the Lord our God, the Lord is One.' This is graven, like the commandments, upon the hearts of the Israelites, and is continuously repeated as the simple, clear expression of the abiding faith of all Jews in all circumstances – even unto death by torture (as in the Inquisition) to force them to renounce their faith. All these issues, as

136

proclaimed, reminded and repeated by Moses throughout his abjuration to the children of Israel, are taken into the religion of Judaism, to be ever harkened back to that memorable final address. It was a most remarkable action of a doughty leader, condemned to death by an ungrateful Yahweh, to perform this last great act. He was totally concerned with the future of his people, on whom he lavished his care for over 40 years, above his own personal situation. Despite the flat refusal of his final plea to Yahweh to be allowed to set foot in the Promised Land, he will now go over every possible detail, to ensure that all is made clear to each and every member of his vast community, extended now to well over 2 million souls. This is a great personal self-sacrifice of a truly great leader, who maintained his total devotion to his duty to his people and his God to the bitter end, continuously praising the very God who has repaid his devoted service so infamously.

The question arises as to why the long repetition of Moses' address and all the details concerning behaviour, habits, punishments, struggles and battles needed to be largely repeated in Leviticus and Deuteronomy, having already been qualified (and quantified) in Exodus and Numbers. This surely points to my belief that these extra two books were added as an extension to J's original version, by later writers who sought 'to get in on the action' and take unto themselves some of the creative value of J's unique production. Such alterations as changing Mount Sinai with all its tremendous scenes from the mountain peaks to the valleys below, to neighbouring Horeb, which does not fit well into the story, having a different significance of its own, only serve to show up in sharp relief the lower quality and lack of originality of these following authors. All the evidence so far produced shows clearly the different natures, concepts and versions of the various authors concerned. It becomes apparent that all roads lead directly, or through devious side-paths, back to J's original version. Even the final composite mixture by the Redactor, an Aaronite priest (possibly Ezra), cannot but bow to the inevitable truth, that all J's successors are but copyists, with but little extra to add.

It is left to D to indicate whether he be Hilkiah, the priest who 'discovered' the Scroll of the Law amongst the debris of the Temple just at the right moment to benefit good King Josiah, as foundation for his renewal of the faith and return to their true religion, or Jeremiah, that great, fearless prophet of the truth. Hence the carefully detailed record there of all of Moses' final great oratory, including every commandment and injunction to the Israelites on the brink of entry to Canaan. What, however, is not clear, is what finally happened to all those released from slavery in Egypt only to be condemned by Yahweh, their saviour, after long years of deprivation, wandering like nomads, interminably battling against human foes and those of hunger and thirst – to die in that vast, soul-destroying Wilderness.

We are not left in any doubt about the tragic fate of Moses and Aaron. But there seems to be an omission concerning the final death of all those Israelites, condemned by a remorseless Yahweh to die along the way, before reaching entry to that so often Promised Land, flowing with milk and honey. Moses died at 120 years, so most of the people of the Exodus must have been well advanced in age, with children and grandchildren. Yahweh condemns their 'carcases' to be buried, but we are given no details by any author of where or when. Nor have any discoveries ever been made of mass graves or possessions or memorials. Nothing has surfaced so far to prove or disprove any of the versions which make up the history of the Bible.

There is further curious lack of information about the children who actually qualify to enter the Promised Land, their ages, education, training, tribal situation. What happened to their parents? Were they killed off at a stroke by Yahweh, as with Moses? What was the relationship between doomed parents and their children, on learning that their parents would not be allowed to accompany them? The Bible states they were exterminated by Yahweh as with the Flood and other destructive death-dealing acts. So much time and space is taken up with so many repetitions of all the incidents on the long journey, but none to a description of the upbringing, training and development of the children, due to become Joshua's men of war for all the battles ahead. There is so much important information missing, and so many gaps in these final chapters, that one wonders about Joshua's resources and preparations, so necessary for the major, hazardous task facing him as the new leader. J's successors failed to notice this omission.

We do not learn in those splendid passages in Leviticus and Deuteronomy, just who is being addressed by Moses and Yahweh. Are those from Exodus still alive, or are they now addressing the new generation of grown children? Or have they all suddenly vanished without mention and without trace? We are not informed from whom came these trained warriors numbering over 600,000 men-at-arms. There seems to be no discernible clue to the solution of this intriguing, and somewhat unbelievable situation in both books.

We do know that the Redactor's final composite version, some 500 years after J, favoured P's priestly script, including the whole of Leviticus. He also manoeuvred parts of one version into another. Nobody ever dared attempt to alter radically, and carve up other world authors' work into separate versions, and rename them under different titles.

P, the priests' group, decided arbitrarily to produce the Book

139

of Leviticus, thus stamping their position and powers, rights and support from kings and people, for 'fear of the Lord'. They emerge as the most powerful body of all with every detail of their rights, food and clothing to be supplied gratis, with land and housing. Thus becoming the most privileged class, which they have striven ever since to remain. They took over the mantle of Yahweh's authority, and suggested that the whole issue of the Israelites' preparation for, and final entry into, the unknown land of Canaan, was a priestly arrangement and organisation throughout. Hence all the weight of accent on the rôle of priest and the tribe of Levi, with enumeration of their duties, acting for Yahweh, their rights of power and obedience by all the people. They seemed more concerned with the people's duties and obligations to them, than their reason for being chosen, namely to SERVE Yahweh and his people. We witness the lesson and example of the corruption of power, even among the priests who carried on their own internecine power struggle for predominance of Aaronites against Mushites.

Perhaps there is a clue in Deuteronomy 7:12: 'the Lord thy God shall keep with thee the covenant and the mercy which he sware unto thy fathers'. These are not the words of J, who emphasised the breaking of those covenants and merciless treatment by Yahweh. It becomes obvious that parts of both Leviticus and Deuteronomy were added by different hands attempting to tone down his stark reality. But they cannot hide J's Yahweh, as in Deuteronomy 8:2-3. 'And thou shalt remember all the ways which the Lord thy God hath led thee these forty years in the wilderness, and he humbled thee and suffered thee to hunger, and fed thee with manna, which thou knewest not... that he might make thee know that man doth not live by bread only, but by every thing that proceedeth out of the mouth of the Lord doth man live.' They still must move from Yahweh's boasts to his continuous threats: 'And it shall be, if thou shalt forget the Lord thy God, and walk after other gods, and serve them, and worship them, I testify against you this day that ye shall surely perish.' (Deuteronomy 8:19). Here is the real Yahweh, the true original of J.

However much the priests and rabbis later tried desperately to rid themselves of this realist J, even to forbidding the use of the original YHVH (pronounced Yahweh), by changing to Adonai (and later Jehovah), and interpreting in more earthly mode as the 'Lord our God', a man-made, watered-down version of Yahweh, that dynamic anthropomorphic Creator (and destroyer), they cannot rid themselves of J's original version. Yahweh keeps returning and retaining his formation rôle, despite all their efforts to alienate and remove him from close contact with mankind. Though they later succeed in re-drafting much of the Original Testament and interposing themselves as his voice and his interpreters, with all the power this allows them to assume, the old Yahweh keeps re-appearing, despite the Redactor's efforts.

We are still left without information as to how all those elderly Israelites were killed off before Canaan. Even Moses' lengthy address in Deuteronomy, as in Numbers, keeps reminding them all of their past 40 years in the wilderness. Had Yahweh exterminated the elders (as he did in one fell swoop in the Flood, Sodom, etc), Moses would now be addressing their children and grandchildren, who would not have had all that experience. There are so many gaps and missing details of information that it all seems a most hurried last-minute operation to get rid quickly of Moses and Aaron, and then mysteriously eliminate those condemned ex-slaves after all their sufferings. This would then clear the way for the new chapter of events with the entry at last into Canaan, a huge expanse of land and desert, occupied by many constantly warring tribes and different peoples. Some are even descended

141

from the original Esau and Cain, as also from Lot's illegally
begotten sons, who have produced the ill-favoured Ammonites
and Moabites, who cause their relatives much trouble.

What of the children? We know not how they have been
taught and trained and conditioned. What efforts have the
priests made, and how did they take the news that their
parents were condemned to death and unable to accompany
them into the Promised Land? Would they not have protested
vociferously? We know they were not cowed into sheep-like
obedience, from their conduct later. Joshua needed trained
warriors numbering at least 600,000. Such training would need
to be long and arduous – not easy on a prolonged diet of
manna, scarcely body-building. There are so many issues left
unsolved that one wonders about all the preparations necessary to protect this amorphous mass of well over 2 million
souls about to be sent into the great unknown, with all their
families, young children and possessions. Their new leader
Joshua was taking on multitudinous problems, needing
tremendous courage and powers of leadership, in which he
was fortunate to receive instruction from Moses himself.

As he draws near the end of his peroration, Moses brings the
elders into the action as in chapter 27, enumerating also the
leaders of the tribes, who are to 'stand upon mount Gerizim
to bless the people, when ye are passed over the Jordan:
Simon and Levi, and Judah and Issachar, and Joseph and
Benjamin.' Then the peculiar decision to have the remaining
tribal leaders take up position on mount Ebal for the curses...
'Cursed be the man that maketh a graven or molten image...
cursed be he that dishonoureth his father or his mother.'
Curses for those who do not follow the Commandments – a
curious twist in warnings to the people, showing obvious
mistrust, using both positive and negative, for double pressure
to ensure full intimidation.

In chapter 29, Moses reiterates the actions taken against Pharaoh, then says curiously: 'But the Lord hath not given you a heart to know, and eyes to see, and ears to hear, unto this day. And I have led you forty years in the wilderness; your clothes are not waxen old upon you, and thy shoe is not waxen old upon thy foot'... 'And when ye came unto this place Sihon, the King of Heshbon and Og, the King of Bashan, came out against us into battle, and we smote them.' (Deuteronomy 29:3–6) After this long peroration Moses refers again to the Commandments he had repeated to them, saying: 'For this commandment, which I command thee this day, it is not too hard for thee, neither is it far off.' (modern 'way out') (Deuteronomy 30:11)

'And the Lord said unto Moses: Behold, thy days approach that thou must die; call Joshua... that I may give him a charge.' (Deuteronomy 31:14) After this abrupt dismissal for his services, Yahweh then astonishingly tells Moses to compose a song, after recording everything in a book to hand to the Levites, to be placed in the Ark of the Covenant. Unfortunately as we know, the Ark and the Temple were destroyed at enemy hands – so no written record survived. But this final beautiful song of Moses in verse 32, 'Give ear, ye heavens, and I will speak; and let the earth hear the words of my mouth...' is the final farewell of this, their greatest leader, this quiet, faithful servant of his people, whose name and great compassion and guidance live on for ever, as an example to all the leaders of the world, if only they would follow and emulate him. Alas, most of his successors, right through history to modern times, are too taken up with their own self-aggrandisement to care, as Moses did, for ALL the people.

Finally, Moses blessed all the tribes individually. Then he was allowed by Yahweh to go from the plains of Moab to the top of Mount Pisgah to be shown the Promised Land: 'And the

143

Lord said unto him, This is the land which I sware unto Abraham, unto Isaac, and unto Jacob... I have caused thee to see it with thine eyes, but thou shalt not go over thither.' (Deuteronomy 34:4). That was Yahweh's sole concession to his most faithful servant – to let him die in sight of the Promised Land for which he had worn himself out in daily toil, to bring his people through 40 hard years, but is finally denied access. Even worse was to follow: 'So Moses the servant of the Lord died there in the land of Moab.... And he buried him in the valley... but no man knoweth of his sepulchre unto this day.' (Deuteronomy 34:5–6) We are told 'his eye was not dim, nor his natural force abated'. He was simply removed and extinguished to make way for Joshua, already chosen as his successor.

This is so clearly J's conclusion of his epic of Moses and Exodus that one wonders why later contributors to the Old Testament thought it necessary to break his one, long, continuous account into the final setting of the five books, giving each a distinctive title. Genesis and Exodus make good sense, Numbers, containing all those long lists of 'begats', is well-chosen to break a boring sequence from J's original, and give it a separating chapter. Leviticus we can understand as the desire of the priests to make their establishment, duties, power and prestige clear for all the people to comprehend. Above all, to establish the duties of the people to their priests, which they made complicated, heavy and onerous. But there can be no salient reason to split off Deuteronomy as a separate book from Exodus. It is so obviously just an extension and a repeat of much that has gone before, that it could only have been done by a later writer, eager to establish himself in the hierarchy.

All in all, one is still left wondering how much, after the 'Prologue', from the Beginning to Babel, which is now proven to be mainly myth-based, should now be accepted as the serious history and religion of Judaism. How much did J and others owe to the ancient sagas and fables of oral tradition, or how much was gleaned and gathered from the folklore of other countries? There are as yet no written scrolls, documents or records discovered to prove the authenticity of those first and most important five books, on which the whole history of Judaism, Christianity and Islam finally depend. So we are left with our truly great, original J (and successors), to decide for ourselves what we may believe or accept or refute.

8

DAVID'S STORY: The Rise and Fall of a Great Dynasty

Scion of the tribe of Judah, he reaches instant fame with one heroic act, from shepherd boy to people's hero. Goliath, a massive giant, champion of the Israelites' worst enemy, the mighty Philistines, bellows his challenge seven times for single combat. All Saul's mighty army refuse the repeated challenge, to be decried as cowards. But only Saul has armour like Goliath, to be offered to his champion (who became the origin of our knights who later appeared as champions in the lists), but refused as too big, heavy and cumbersome.

So young David faces him unarmed, having refused the heavy armour offered by King Saul. Goliath and all the Philistines roar with laughter and contempt at the sight of this slender youngster, daring to offer combat to their mighty champion. Calmly undeterred, brave David coolly selects five smooth, sharp stones, testing each carefully to fit his sling, well-used in his work to fend off wild animals. It is said that Goliath had four mighty brothers, hence the extra pebbles.

Goliath peers down at this young lightly-clad boy and sneers at the Israelite warriors: 'Is this the best you can do? I could eat him for breakfast.' David quietly selects his stone, fits it into his sling and with one mighty swing, hurls it straight and true, penetrating Goliath's eye and killing him stone-dead. The Philistines, appalled at this seeming magic, give up the fight and retreat. Despite his youth, David's courageous act transforms him, in one fell swing, from unknown shepherd boy to Israel's champion. David, youngest son of Jesse, has thus signed his name into Israel's long, heroic history.

Saul now takes the young hero into his own family, to be entertained by his further proficiency in song and music from his harp and poetry, practised by David in his lonely vigils guarding his sheep. Saul's son Jonathan becomes his lifelong friend and companion. But Saul grows jealous of David's skill and accomplishments, and increasing military fame as he matures. In his mad rages he seeks to kill David, who yet tries to soothe him with his music, and quieten his fits of wild temper.

Eventually Saul's rages increase to such an extent that David has to flee for his life, with J's neat little story of his narrow escape from death at the hands of Saul's assassination team by sliding down from a rear window with the aid of his wife. Hunted by Saul, David gathers together men from his own tribe of Judah and friends, and then takes refuge in the hills. Another clever touch of J's is the incident where weary Saul sleeps in a cave, unaware that David is hidden in its dark recesses. David has therefore an easy target and could have dispatched Saul, but has mercy on him as King, just letting him know how near he was to death at the hands of the one he so relentlessly pursued, by cutting off a piece of his robe and removing his spear.

Saul realises his mad folly and seeks to mend his ways. But his manic depression worsens and he eventually resorts to the forbidden exorcising of the dead prophet Samuel. The Witch of Endor performs this forbidden rite of witchcraft for the insistent, demanding Saul, and eventually Samuel rises from Sheol, the resting place of the dead. He repudiates Saul and prophesies his early death and that of his family, and the rise of David to become King of all Israel. But, on Saul's death, his surviving son Ishbal becomes King, only soon to be assassinated, leaving David, already crowned King of Judah, now to be crowned King of all Israel.

David (1000–961 BC) is the equivalent of the Sumerian version of the ideal shepherd, brave, imaginative, sensible and immensely capable. He unites the monarchy as consecrated King and leader. He was indeed a mighty warrior and doughty leader. He twice defeated their worst and fiercest enemy, the Philistines, even though he had been on friendly terms with them when escaping Saul. Then he captured Jerusalem, making it his capital city, to become famous throughout history as Israel's Holy City, beloved of all. It became the hope and watchword of the Jews in exile, and is always remembered in their prayers.

David's kingdom was extended through well-planned battles and victories, for that whole area was continuously at war through consuming jealousy, greed and hatred. He succeeded in defeating all his enemies and extended his empire from the Nile to the Euphrates, including Lebanon and Syria. By creating good relations with the Phoenicians, especially King Hiram of Tyre, they served him well as established sailors and merchant men, bringing him goods, gold, silver, materials and spices from many lands. It is said they even brought back tin from Cornwall on visits to England, where they founded a small colony.

Israel, for the first time in history, now became not only an established state, but also a widespread empire, ruled over by a wise, powerful, inspiring leader whose personal charm captivated all who met him. There were also extensive dependencies giving access to valuable natural and mineral sources, including copper from conquered Edam. His people enjoyed a

148

higher standard of living, with better education and culture under their strong leader. David also renewed their religious faith, personally demonstrating his own faith and joy in his worship of Yahweh, by dancing (the Israelites' natural expression of joy or happiness or celebration), before the Ark in the tabernacle, and by composing songs and psalms of praise.

At the same time he created a big, standing army of mercenaries who served him faithfully, in addition to his own regular soldiers (2 Samuel 8). The state waxed strong, secure and wealthy, and much respected under him. But, as a man, he also had his personal weaknesses. He lusted after Bathsheba, sending her husband Uriah, the Hittite captain, to his death in battle. Nathan the prophet condemned David, and he had to suffer the death of his beloved son Absalom, who had murdered his own brother Amnon for the wrong he had done to his sister Tamar. Absalom had sought to take over from his father, marching on Jerusalem, only to be routed and killed by General Joab. David went barefoot in mourning the loss of his favourite son: 'O my son Absalom, my son Absalom! Would I had died for thee, O Absalom, my son, my son.' (2 Samuel 1)

The city of Jerusalem, won in mighty battle, was David's personal establishment and his great heirloom to the Jewish people and mankind, always to be regarded as David's Holy City, life-centre of Israel. He was undoubtedly a unique commanding world figure, setting the example of heroic leader with supreme manly, law-abiding and religious qualities, admired and respected by all. He possessed vitality and the qualities of leadership, with great personal charm and magnetism, attracting affection and loyalty, with abiding faith in himself and all his people and his God.

David's astounding energy and vitality stem from marriage mix, first from the ever loyal Ruth the Moabite who captivated Boaz, who fathered Jesse, father of David, and also from Tamar the Canaanite. Her indomitable urge to become inheritor of the blessing, is frustrated by the sickliness and lack of vitality of Judah's three sons. As widow of sickly Er and weakly Onan, leaving only the useless Shelah – even if Judah had not disobeyed the ancient Hebrew custom of Yibbum (surviving brother of deceased husband to marry widow). The boldness and resourcefulness of the wronged Tamar is quite startling, for she is fearless and determined with all the courage J so admired in his heroines, rising above adversity.

Judah's wife dies. Judah, her father-in-law, goes to Timnath for the sheep-shearing. Tamar, dressed and veiled overall as a prostitute, sits by the wayside to lure Judah on his way. Her plan succeeds fully, and Tamar demands his seal and crook as pledges of future payment. But when Judah sends his clerk to redeem them, the woman is no longer there. Tamar now proves her case in court that Judah must now marry her legally. This he does perforce, and she gives birth to two sons, one of whom, Peretz, becomes an ancestor of David. Thus Tamar guarantees the heritage of vitality of David, gaining herself a main position in Jewish history, into which she was not born but created for herself, with courage and determination. Here is evidence of the cunning hand of this great author J, who keeps us spellbound with his intricate plots and unexpected twists and turns. No wonder David is his great hero. He sees to all the elements of David's parentage himself, gaining our admiration for his Shakespeare – like weaving of his intricate plots. As with his Yahweh and his kings and prophets, we never know what will be finally revealed on the other side, for he is a master of concealed plots and twists of scene.

It is remarkable that Saul, David and Jonathan all fathered children with Baal in their names. Baal is even likened to

Yahweh by a priestly scribe. So this ancient god Baal was also a household name with the Hebrews and Israelites. King Hosiah was the first to show real antipathy to Baal usage. It is remarkable how these ancient primitive gods continued their influence well beyond the 10th century BC, despite the ever-growing strength of the monotheistic God Yahweh.

David's great, hard-won united kingdom passed from his power, security and affluence after his death, from the end of Solomon's reign in 922 to the fall of Jerusalem in 587, through family split, to division of power and gradual decline and final extinction as an independent political entity in some 350 years, marking the end of the greatest period in Jewish history. Nathan the prophet and Zadok, the Aaronite priest, both sponsored Solomon, son of Bathsheba (David's favourite wife), as successor to the throne, opposing his elder brother Adonijah. Solomon promptly had Adonijah killed, and also David's faithful General Jaob, for no valid reason. So many of the good qualities promoted and developed by David were quickly reduced, and many changes wrought. The Israelites meantime learnt good farming virtues from the Canaanites, long-established as farmers, whilst the Israelites were forced to live all those generative years as nomads. In addition, however, they also began again to worship the Canaan gods Baal, god of nature, and Astarte, goddess of fertility, love and war, arousing the anger of Yahweh.

Solomon's wisdom was far-famed, and his courts were always well-attended to hear his pearls of wisdom. He established friendly relations with many countries, in direct contrast to the hitherto continuous battling in defence or attack of all his predecessors. He cleverly selected royal princesses as wives, and vastly exaggerated rumours credited him with 700 wives and 300 concubines, a situation beyond man's comprehension. He was actually attributed some 38 wives and 24 concubines.

More than enough, for he had to have his friend King Hiram of Tyre build a mighty big palace to house them all. His Temple (again built by the Phoenicians) took seven years to build, but his greater-sized palace took 13 years. If only these far-famed edifices had been preserved!

Great and wise though he was, he still could not match his great father, David. Solomon had his own personal weakness, including a love of grandeur, pomp and ceremony – as with the now world-famous visit of the Queen of Sheba. But his greed and incessant love of finery – gold, silver, precious jewels, silks and fine materials and luxury led to insupportable costs heavily owed to Hiram and his Phoenicians. He imposed harsh taxes and pursued a severely autocratic rule, even forcing all his subjects, of whatever rank, to serve one month's labour per annum, without pay or reward. The love, affection and loyalty, which David deservedly won from all his people by personal example, was lost by Solomon. He found himself in such huge debt to Hiram of Tyre that he had to trade off some cities against his debts. He not only had individual shrines built for his several wives to worship as their own custom, but even began to worship some of these 'graven images' himself. He neglected latterly many of his duties, extracting so much unlawfully from his people that he lost their love and affection and all the respect and admiration they undoubtedly had in his early years of just, wise rule.

Interestingly, there is no mention of statues, carvings, paintings and works of art in all the years of the ancient Hebrews become Israelites. Not only were they forbidden to build any 'images' (remember Aaron's golden calf at Sinai?), but there was never time to devote to the arts, for they were 'eternally busy' and on the move. That is why their feelings and sentiments are devoted to the written word, at which they became famously efficient, producing the first alphabet, copied by

Phoenicians and Greeks – from Hebrew Aleph Bet; Greek alpha, beta; English a, b.

Solomon even neglected the education of his own sons and the training necessary to fill the rôle of king. Consequently, on his death in 922, not only was much of his kingdom heavily mortgaged, but he left his sons quarrelling over their rights to the kingdom. Hence the split, with 'Israel' including ten tribes in the north, and David's tribe Judah (alone) in the south centred on Jerusalem, thus demonstrating the truth of the adage 'a house divided...'. Solomon was the great supporter of the Aaronite priests, choosing Zadok (who had given him much help in his succession) as his High Priest. But he expelled the Mushite leading priest Abiathar back to Shiloh and forbade him to enter Jerusalem.

David did not deserve the bad behaviour, infidelity and, above all, the weakness of so many of his descendants. They betrayed him on all counts: religion and faithfulness to Yahweh above all, thus breaking the covenant of Yahweh with David, promising unbroken succession for his family. Also breaking the commandments of Moses' Torah, and the centralisation of religion of the One God at Jerusalem. All lost in the final extermination of his family line, with all his great empire swept away.

There is no doubt that David was J's real hero. J admires and relates to him as hero, with none of the usual quirks or sudden displays of wrath by Yahweh. Obviously for J, David was the ideal man, leader and king. From his grandson's court in Jerusalem, J had a ringside seat to watch the downfall of Northern Israel, no doubt uneasily wondering when it would be their turn. How he must have wished for a second David. Indeed from then on, all Jews longed for the return of David, and expected his eventual return in the garb of the Messiah,

153

to save them from their never-ending enemies and bring universal peace at last. Maybe he is resting in Sheol, awaiting the right moment for his recall.

Whatever primary inspiration J may have drawn from the Sumerians and others, he surpassed them all with his biblical delineation of his greatest characters, who live on in Jewish and world history. David was the greatest and most devoted king and leader of all times. He brought his still separate and undisciplined people together to the peak of greatness, establishing his Era as a period of literary achievement. Psalms, Song of Songs, 2 Samuel, Proverbs: the books of J reach the sublime heights of Hebrew imagination and creative composition, which have never been surpassed.

9

THE CODE OF THE BIBLE – WITH REFLECTIONS ON KABBALA

The Book of Genesis and the Letter Code, claimed by Kabbala to indicate the ancient mythical Hebrew wisdom

Orthodox Hebrew, Christian and Moslem religious thinking all stem from the Bible. Others deem most of Genesis and the other four books to be based on myths and ancient folklore. Kabbala maintains that the Pentateuch was written in a specific code which cannot be deciphered without full decryptic knowledge of the cipher and its keys, still undiscovered, although Kabbalists advance different solutions.

Each letter of the Hebrew alphabet represents a specific number, of special significance beyond its arithmetical value. Each letter also has its own intrinsic strength and meaning. Kabbalists claim that these 22 letters of the Hebrew alphabet, which have remained identically the same since originated c 3250 BC, represent the interplay of the natural energies, which are universal. Rabbinical views maintain that nothing in Genesis is there by mere chance. It all depends on finding the solution to this supposed, but unrevealed, secret code, for the true meaning to be revealed. As a cryptologist, it seems doubtful to me.

The first actual known code simply involved reversing the Hebrew alphabet, as a substitution code called Atbash, later adopted by the Romans as their Caesar code. This fact must cast further doubt on claims of the existence of such an intricate earlier code. More important would be to discover why the 22 letters (without any vowels) are also proper names as well as numbers. This makes the Hebrew alphabet unique in treble significance. Perhaps a more sensible approach would be to try to discover the hidden values and concepts of the legends, myths, fables and folklore of those ancient times, recorded by different countries. The great quantities of clay tablets and records so far discovered, originating from so many different areas around Mesopotamia, show a remarkably close inter-connection.

The 22 letters composing the alphabet are the initials of names and individual meanings long lost, but given suggested interpretation by Kabbalists. They cannot simply be transposed by A, B, C for Aleph, Beth, Gimel, or by use of conventional words to describe objects or matters of special significance. Kabbalists claim that the Book of Genesis was originally a Kabbalistic script, tracing its source back to times immemorial, full of ancient history and sagas. But they have not yet been able to decipher what they claim to be their own secret script. Thus their contentions are unproven. The personification of a God who 'begins' a creation, they say, is but a futile attempt to explain the real mystery which lies in the engendering of time, space and life, the essence of 'being'. Scientists would agree with such a rendering.

Kabbala claims to have existed before Abraham. But more modern developments, since its 19th-century renewal, have made it now unique unto itself as a way of thinking, based on what they esteem reasoned developments, which lead to a different interpretation of the Bible. Thus they interpret names differently. Original Abram becomes Ab-ram, the father of Ram. In Egypt, Eastern and Indo-European countries, Ram denotes the universal spirit as 'foundation of the world'. Likewise for the Druids, their ancient worship of stones (as in Aylesbury and Stonehenge), expressed that same spirit. There is a good example of this ancient worship of stones in Jacob's story, when Yahweh calls him to leave his scheming father-in-law Laban: 'I am the God of Beth-el, where thou anointedst a pillar.' (Genesis 31:13) When Laban pursues them after Rachel has stolen her father's most precious possession, his household gods (made of stone), they make a covenant of peace between them: 'And Jacob took a stone, and set it up for a pillar... and they took stones and made an heap.... And Laban said this heap is witness between me and thee this day... and Jacob offered a sacrifice in the mountains.' (Genesis 31:45–54) Altars of stone were the earliest form used by our ancient ancestors for prayer, worship and sacrifice.

Even now people everywhere in the world, including Britain and Ireland *et al*, will stand on a stone or kneel for a prayer before a stone altar, like the original stone altars of our ancestors. Or even a wish, as with the Blarney Stone or wishing well. The very first forms of pictorial design were scratched on stone. The stone tablets of the Law signified the everlasting strength of stone. Early Kabbala and other writers seem to me to have missed the full significance of stone and its influence on our lives from the earliest 'Stone Age'. There is so much more to discover in the history of our world beyond the simple presentation of the facts. At least the Kabbalists strive to unlock the significance of these ancient events, whilst still missing mankind's close and enduring relations with stone, which seems to bear an eternal meaning all its own.

Kabbala avers that the intent of the Bible story differs from the normally accepted interpretation. They translate 'Ur of the Chaldees' as Aur Kasdeem, meaning 'light of the magicians'. Thus the Kasdeems (truly strange people who came originally from the East to inhabit Sumer), were astrologers, diviners, magicians and mathematicians. They were also matter-of-fact, inventive people, very much concerned with the material things of everyday life, inventing the very first cuneiform sign script, which they duly recorded on clay tablets, copied by their neighbours, who grew greedily jealous of their great success and wealth, invention of wheel and plough and money, and construction of advanced houses and even schools. So, as was the way in those regions, their neighbours just had to destroy them. Ur was burnt to the ground after Abraham left with his father and family. A most intriguing 'black-haired' inventive people, full of wisdom, who might well have been our good and worthy ancestors had they been left to develop in peace.

Abram freed himself from their special gods of nature, declaring himself the first monotheist and follower of Yahweh. He continued his life successfully and normally until he received instructions from Yahweh (direct), to move to Canaan to behold the land promised by Yahweh to be his inheritance, for the great nation he was to engender. Then everything changed and Abram became Abraham, meaning Father of All Nations. Once the great future was ordained and revealed to him by Yahweh, his life became recharged. He was given insight into the future planned for his people, with their unique religion, his descendants waxing strong and mighty. Such vision of the future for his own family development was given to no other man throughout history. The witness of the violent destruction of Sodom and Gomorrah, in the company of Yahweh and his messengers, must have affected him profoundly – not pursued by Bible or Kabbala. Further tempestual mass destruction by Yahweh himself, of his own creatures and creation. How could he have allowed so much sinfulness among his own creatures to bring him yet again to such total destruction? It seems inexplicable, but it was to recur again and again through thousands of years, including our wars, depriving millions of their fundamental right to life.

There is no clue nor explanation of why Abraham had to wait for his son until he reached 100 (he was 75 when called to leave Ur), with Sarai his wife so ashamed of being barren that she even gave him Hagar, her Egyptian maid, to bear him a son, Ishmael, who founded a great nation. If Yahweh were planning this mighty nation of his 'Chosen People' to come from Abraham, why did he have to wait so agonisingly long, that poor old Sarai laughed in his face at his so late promise to her husband? Yahweh, apparently upset at Sarai's mocking laughter, sets out to prove to her his capability in producing Isaac, by his own effort, as with Eve from Adam.

Abraham passes his blessing (claimed to be the significant meaning of Kabbala – to receive), to his son Isaac, who bestows Yahweh's blessing on Jacob, the trickster younger son, disguised to deceive his father and rob his brother of his rightful inheritance. Jacob, however, gives preference to Joseph, his eleventh son, over his eldest son. Once again we have the strange attempted murder of Yahweh's chosen one, instigated by Yahweh himself. First Isaac ordered to be sacrificed by his own father, then Jacob, and then Joseph cast into a pit to die, only to be rescued by strangers. These strange treatments, or tests, are to continue seemingly with all those champions chosen by Yahweh, to gauge their strength and ability to be worthy of his trust. Kabbala only avers that these are such tests of ability and confidence, but advances no viable explanation, nor do the biblical authors.

All the characters in what I call J's Prologue, from Creation and Adam and Eve to Noah and the deadly Flood, prove to be mythical archetypes, not real historical persons. Each finds

159

his close or near resemblance in almost identical folklore pre-written in legends of Sumeria, Akkadia, Assyria, Babylonia, the Hittites and worldwide. It took until the 10th century BC for a unique, but anonymous, original author, known only as J, to weave into his timeless web such intriguing stories and characters who have lived and endured through all the strife and turbulence of the ensuing thousands of years. But he and his successors reveal no knowledge of Kabbala, which claims to have been already in existence and passed to Moses at Sinai.

After Noah and the world-destroying Flood comes J's ironic humorous diversion of the curious episode of Babel, to lighten the depression, by relating the tale of man's overweening ambition to become godlike in self-assertion. As also the significance of the myriad different languages, resulting from Yahweh's mischievous demolition of that pyramid or Ziggurat construction, raised by ambitious humans seeking to reach the heavens. There are many similar erections by Incas, Aztecs and many others to penetrate the heavens for unrevealed reasons. Everything important has to happen atop the mountains, especially Sinai. Important people were buried on hills and mountain tops, hence the discovery of so many graves there and in barrows. Death was described as 'reaching one's mountain'. Merlin, Bruce Barbarossa, David were all interred atop of mountains to reappear at their right time.

After this entertaining Prologue comes the serious beginning of the history and religious development of the Hebrews into Israelites and Judaism. This new Beginning commences with Abraham, now dubbed Father of All Nations. As the first true monotheist he acknowledges Yahweh as his Supreme God, to be obeyed and followed at all times.

His grandson Jacob is then transformed into Israel, holding

160

fast to Yahweh, to bring forth the planned great nation to be called the Children of Israel, to shape the destiny of his people. The Patriarchs' major mission is to engender the seeds from which will grow the great world nations of Jews, Christians and Muslims (from Abraham's son Ishmael). Theirs is the simpler rôle, to set forth the Beginning of the three great nations, and a religion stretching world-wide into the future. Yet there remains a myth-like quality in this, the first Family: Abraham has to witness the total destruction of Sodom and Gomorrah by fire and water (after Yahweh's rainbow Covenant with Noah, never again to destroy by the world by drowning). Isaac plays a quieter rôle, between the incident of his own strange origin and the equally strange birth of his twin sons, Esau and Jacob. It is the birth of ambitious Jacob, which presages the future development of Israel. Kabbala sees Jacob as 'Hereditary Man'.

There follows the legendary tale of Joseph the dreamer. He survives the attempted murder by his jealous brothers, to interpret Pharaoh's dreams, and thereby rises to supreme power. Joseph receives the blessing from Jacob, and his family and all their offspring receive the benefit. Before him Genesis concentrated on the family unit. With Joseph was born a people and a nation. Because of Joseph, the Children of Israel were fruitful and increased abundantly. The more they were afflicted later, 'the more they multiplied and grew'. Yet the mystery remains, why did Yahweh permit the reduction of his people from great prosperity to harsh bondage and rough treatment over hundreds of years under succeeding Pharaohs? Unless this might be another of those extraordinary tests of J's Yahweh, to find out whether the strength of his Chosen People was sturdy and resilient enough to withstand the severity of later Pharaohs before being rescued.

It is noteworthy that Joseph's story is matched closely by the

161

Egyptian tale of the two brothers who fell out over the sexual demands of one wife on her brother-in-law, loyally refused by him. He then had to flee for his life, until the truth was revealed. This casts doubt on the originality and authenticity of J's Joseph story. But the Kabbala is more intent on the line of descent from Abraham, maintained in direct bloodline, using those hundreds of years in Egypt to grow and wax great, as an expanded family. There were some 70 persons in Jacob's family on first arrival in Egypt about 1700 BC. At Exodus, we are told of 600,000 men plus women and children, with all their belongings and Egyptian gifts to speed them on their way.

Most religions arise out of mysterious antecedents and develop with the advent of strong leaders. Judaism began from the ancient myths, fables, folklore and beliefs inherited from their primitive ancestors, who first worshipped the sun, moon, fire and personified gods of nature. Primitive mankind needed to worship something beyond itself, but in tangible form. Hence the early gods, especially of fertility and nature, and even individual 'household gods', usually carved from stone, to guard the safety and sanctity of the home and family – not only from marauders but also from the 'evil one', always threatening, especially by night.

The Kabbala set forth this belief in symbols, derived from their judgement of the characters and events described in the Bible (according to J and other writers) and the Prophets. Kabbalists attribute most to the Tree of Life, neglected in Genesis' description of the events in Eden. They concentrate on the relationship of its various parts and connections, from the Crown at its head, pointing heavenwards, to its roots firmly embedded in the good earth. They pose the important question: why concentrate on the tasting of the forbidden fruit of the Tree of Knowledge, seeking equality with Yahweh?

162

Why did they not eat first of the fruit of the Tree of Life, which would then have gained them immortality? The real reason for the stark, harsh, bitter judgement imposed on these first mortals by Yahweh for gaining forbidden knowledge, may well have been a hasty decision to move them forthwith from Eden, so as to avoid any danger of their gaining immortality from the Tree of Life, to vex him for ever.

The fantastic story of Moses has also a myth-like Beginning. The story, we are led to believe, begins with the brutal edict of harsh Pharaoh, to reduce the continuous upsurge of the Hebrews by slaughtering their first-born sons. When this scheme fails, he orders general onslaught of males by his soldiers. One mother of the tribe of Levi floats her son, in a well-caulked basket, in the bulrushes, watched over by his sister. Pharaoh's daughter rescues the boy and adopts him. So he becomes Prince Ra-Mose. But we are told nothing of his upbringing, education or training.

Unfortunately, this lovely, fairy-tale beginning is rather spoilt by the knowledge that there already existed at least one other similar watery childhood rescue, that of King Sargon the Great, who also survived his basket floating down the Euphrates, to achieve greatness. J tells us nothing of Moses' growth to manhood. We are left to surmise how his family somehow kept contact, so that he was aware of his true background. Hence his pity and anger evoked by the brutal treatment of his own people by the vicious Egyptian taskmasters. J omits any description of Moses' years in Pharaoh's family, or details of discovery of the murdered taskmaster's hidden body. J does not waste words unnecessarily. He remains close to his principal story, leaving out unnecessary details sought by his readers. But Moses must surely have been taught some of the qualities necessary to develop for leadership by Pharaoh's staff, to be put to good use in Exodus.

J obviously decides to plunge Moses *in media res* at this juncture. He flees into the barren Sinai desert and, against expectations, survives. The burning bush incident at Hebron marks the real beginning of Moses' greatest task, to weld this amorphous mass into a homogenous entity. When Moses enquired at Horeb (Exodus 3:2–13): 'What shall I say to them is his name?' the reply came from the burning bush: 'Aleph-Hay-Yod-Hay': 'I am what I am, I am what I will be.' This, according to Kabbala, describes the life-death-life-death continuous interplay between Yahweh and mankind. They maintain that Moses knew Kabbala from oral inheritance, hence his ability to overcome great problems. To me it sums up in one pithy sentence the basic philosophy of life.

Exodus 20:13 reiterates the major command: 'Thou shalt not kill', so often commanded by so many guilty killers. This includes Yahweh, who produces the Law yet apparently considers himself above his own law, with his mass murders and wholesale series of destruction. Again, a vivid lesson of reality, repeated ever after; and just as relevant now.

One of the greatest insoluble problems arising out of Exodus, is that of 24:9–11: 'Then went up Moses and Aaron, Nadab and Abihu, and seventy of the elders of Israel; and they saw the God of Israel; and there was under His feet as it were, a paved work of sapphire stone... and also they beheld God, and did eat and drink.' This does not make sense. Exodus 19:11–13: 'The Lord will come down in the sight of all the people upon Mount Sinai'... 'Take heed to yourselves that ye go not up into the mount, or *touch* the border of it: *whosoever toucheth the mount shall be surely put to death*.' It is impossible to reconcile this complete contradiction. It may have been interposed by a later writer or scribe. Further, to state that God has feet presupposes a body like any other god. Yet they have been led to believe their own God, above all, was a

164

Supreme Spirit. Kabbala maintains that the 'sapphire stone' means Sepher, the Book.

It is all an incredible mix, possibly due to an introduction by another writer after J, who gives no record of Yahweh meeting anybody face to face, after Adam, other than his chosen few: Abraham, Jacob and Moses. It is extremely doubtful that there may be any coded significance to this mysterious contradiction, first of the people in Exodus 19:12 being absolutely forbidden even to 'touch the border' of the mount. Then but five verses later (Exodus 24:9–12) up they go, Moses and Aaron, with Nadab and Abihu and also 70 elders, to a feast with God on the mountain. This makes nonsense of the sacred picture so carefully built up of the unseen, unapproachable Supreme Spirit. One wonders how the P (priestly group) and the Redactor and future writers, priests, rabbis could allow it to remain. The Kabbala offers no solution, except possibly the text of letters and their numbers changing the apparent meaning of words when added together in the code.

The Mosaic Code

Primarily the work of two great prophets, Ezra (450–400 BC), believed to have been the Redactor who produced the final version of the five Books, and Jeremiah (650–585 BC), son of Hilkiah the High Priest, who 'discovered' the Torah in the ruins of the temple. King Josiah (647–601 BC) revised the Mosaic Laws with Hilkiah and his prophets, thereby reversing completely the pagan and irreverent deterioration of his people since Solomon's fall from grace. This became a comprehensive code based not only on their monotheistic religion, but also inclusive of all details of personal conduct and hygiene, with lists of permissible or forbidden food, as in Exodus and Deuteronomy.

There was no other code as complete and detailed. The nearest was King Hammurabi's Laws (c 1700 BC) with his code of conduct and judgement, of clear relationship to these later Mosaic Laws. Later followed Dionysus the 'Lawgiver', with his own two tablets of stone, similar to Moses. Finally Zoroaster's Book of the Law. But the Mosaic Code stands for all time, complete in itself and above all others before or since. It has come down through the ages, copied and followed in essence by most countries, including Britain, which boasts the oldest established laws and legal code in the Western hemisphere – finally being somewhat forcefully thrust aside by the new, somewhat bureaucratic European Union seeking to override all well-established systems.

2 Chronicles 36 relates the short reigns of the sons of Josiah. Three months for Jehoahaz, deposed by Egypt, who made his brother Eliakim (becomes Jehoiakim), king. But both 'did that which was evil in the sight of the Lord his God'. So Nebuchadnezzar of Babylon defeated him, and carried him off to Babylon. 'Jehoachim, his son, reigned in his stead.' Only 18 years old, he reigned three months and ten days but did 'that which was evil in the sight of the Lord'. One may ask how an 18-year-old boy could in three months do so much evil that Nebuchadnezzar had to carry him also off to Babylon, making his brother Zedekiah king at 21 years. He managed to last eleven years before doing 'that which was evil in the sight of the Lord his God'. But he also refused to listen to the warnings of Jeremiah, and rebelled against Nebuchadnezzar and Yahweh, in company with the priests and people, and even 'the messengers of God' and 'scoffed at his prophets'. Therefore he brought down upon them the king of the Chaldeans, 'who slew their young men, maidens and the old, destroyed the Temple, and sacked Jerusalem', carrying the remainder off to Babylon for 70 years – until released by Cyrus, King of Persia, who sent them back to Jerusalem.

166

Cyrus sent Nehemiah with the Temple's vessels and money, and an armed guard, to rebuild Jerusalem and the Temple. Ezra, prophet and scribe, brought back the book of the Law of Moses. Ezra is thought to have been the Redactor who made a composite whole of the Pentateuch, from the work and versions of the previous authors and scribes. He purported to have knowledge of the inner working of the Kabbala.

There followed the Greek period, overtaken by the brutal attacks and destruction of the Syrians, eventually defeated by the heroic guerilla tactics of the brave Maccabees family led by Judas, the Hammer. But there was to be no peace for Jerusalem. Continuously under attack until the Roman conquest, Jerusalem was destroyed by Titus in 20 AD. The final death-knell came with Hadrian in 135 AD, followed by the Diaspora dispersing the ill-treated and righteous Jews, who refused to bow to the Romans, to the four corners of the world. Even the Kabbala can find no significant crumb of comfort, or code of explanation or expiation, for those criminal acts against the Jews, nor excuse for the subsequent sins of the world. The position of this brave little nation should now be restored to its full standing as rightfully and properly amongst the world leaders. Jerusalem should be rebuilt, whole and entire, to become again the centre of the world's major religions, in expiation for all the evil done to them by the world, and returned under the care and control of Israel, whose capital it has always rightfully been as the Holy City of David.

From the 2nd century AD the Kabbala became known and followed in almost every part of the world. It is even to be discovered in the Koran. Not surprising, in the knowledge that Mohammed was actually taught by rabbis. Hence the belief that the three great religions of Judaism, Christianity and Islam, should now join together in restoration of mutual roots back to Abraham and, even further, to the neglected original Tree of Life. For that is where any code must begin, as it does with Kabbala. Thus would the divisions fall away, and the world harmony of peace and co-operation be finally achieved.

It is necessary to begin anew with the study of the Bible from a more factual, serious premise. How can such a Beginning situation be accepted as an unknown spiritual something, creating our world and everything therein out of nothing? J at least attempts a better definition, but his also does not stand up to close examination or criticism. An entire religion cannot be conjured up out of myths, ancient folklore and magic. Even the very words and language used, whether Hebrew or English, have too often a double meaning. The changes, alterations and amendments without explanation, cast doubt on which to follow, or whether any be acceptable in present form, in stated or implied meaning.

The Kabbalists seek to decode in their own way the numbers attached to the letters of the Hebrew alphabet. But nobody as yet has been able to solve the puzzle of the real significance of these letter numbers, which appear to be unique then to the Hebrew alphabet. Kabbalists say each number has a meaning relating to cosmic forces. But they do not explain to our understanding the true nature of these cosmic forces, or whether the ancient Hebrews were aware of them. The school of thought in Germany in the 19th century furthered the intention of the rabbis of the 2nd century AD, to transmit Yahweh to some heavenly abode (like the Greek gods), dispensing from on high conventional morality through the priests. Some Kabbalists were known to seek magic formulae, deduced from the letter-code.

168

It is right and proper to study the past, but we do not live in it. Our life and situation are now, and we plan our future in our present knowledge, whether religious, scientific, philosophical or materialistic, based on or deriving from the revelations of the past. We are all creatures of the present, which itself is an ever-moving entity. At the same time, we are inheritors of the ever-increasing scientific knowledge which is changing our outlook and circumstance, and clarifying our understanding and relationship with our past.

The original authors of the Bible were undoubtedly influenced by their past. But they were writing in the light of that knowledge for their present, without consideration of the effect of their script on the far future. So it has been, and so it continues now. We write for our present generation, knowing not how our work and thoughts will be reviewed and considered in the next century, which must itself be subject to its own changes, unless Yahweh decides on another cataclysm. If J were alive now, he might well be considering our present spate of earthquakes, tornadoes, volcanic eruptions, floods and huge rainfalls, even with modern scientific advance, as worthy of new stories of religious or biblical significance. But how would his outlook on Yahweh have changed in the light of present knowledge, and all the different faiths and beliefs, as well as the many faces of present religions, ever-differing and arguing and contending violently within themselves, and with modern science?

Kabbala accepts that the original text deals with the relationship of mankind with Yahweh, as of that time. It maintains that a 'beginning' of time and space is unthinkable, despite modern scientific revelation. Our normal thinking is concerned with 'description' of objects, not with the actual units. Our concept of colour or shades or music calls forth in the listener feelings, images, symbols familiar to our own recollection and capability of imagination. Hence Kabbala postulates that knowledge is a cosmic energy, conveyed by the letter-numbers – an assumption immediately rejected by scientists. They might well argue that transcendence is completely beyond understanding, or even possibility of measure, like timelessness. Our mind acts and reacts according to our thoughts, but does not produce a solution to the basic significance of life. Kabbalists maintain that problem would be resolved by deciphering the letter-code, still incomprehensible. Knowledge of basic keys and settings is needed to decipher any code. The Kabbalists have not yet produced any solutions or even clues to the biblical code they postulate.

However, certain facts reveal the gradual formalising of religions in our time. Most religion has become a ritual, whether Christian, Jewish or Islam. It is set in fixed, prescribed tracks, with repetition becoming accepted in daily or weekly form. It is easy to follow the broad lines, so carefully laid down and ritually taught by each religion's leaders, to a regular prescribed dose. But this is failing to satisfy many thinking people, who cannot relate such unchanging ritual to all the exciting events and discoveries presented to us continuously through modern sources of information. Religious leaders must come to terms with the rapid growth in information, education, thinking processes, expanding with the intake of regular factual information on world as well as local events – or see our churches and religious institutions becoming empty. Many have already closed, others are trying to join or share services and religious and family events.

Young people brought up in all such religions are leaving, dissatisfied with the same old rituals, which do not succeed in marrying into modern conditions. Yet they still seek to find a satisfying, acceptable meaning to life. They need a faith to inspire or sustain their imagination, feelings of insecurity, or

170

vague searching for a viable solution to unsolved, partly understood problems. 'No man is an island' – a faith in something intangible, spiritual, used to be enough to carry one forward. Now a spiritual belief is sought in tandem with modern scientific knowledge and advancement, to allow the interplay of modern devices with an active contribution to an acceptable, sustaining religious cum spiritual belief. Whether in a supreme, benign Spirit over all our world, or a materialistic view of one life with no hereafter. The Kabbala offers no solution to these problems, but refers us back to the original Tree of Life, set in Eden, and apparently ignored or overlooked by all. The Kabbalists begin their study with this original Tree on which they develop mankind's spiritual life and derivation.

Numerical Power of letters of alphabet

Aleph	=	is the life-death principle of being and non-being
Beth	=	means 'dwellings'
Gimel	=	strength and throat and all body openings
Dalet	=	origin, physical existence
Hay	=	universal life and spirit – the soul
Vav	=	fertilising agent which impregnates
Zayn	=	result of impregnation
Heth	=	store of energy and matter
Teth	=	dynamic
Yod	=	1 + 0: total manipulation of 1 to 9, always building in 10s

Hebrew Alphabet

			Corresponding Letters	Numerical Power
א	Alef	1	A	1
ב	Beth	2	B	2
ג	Gimel	3	G	3
ד	Dalet	4	D	4
ה	Hei	5	H	5
ו	Vav	6	W	6
ז	Zayin	7	Z	7
ח	Cheth	8	Ch	8
ט	Teth	9	T	9
י	Yod	10	Y	10
כ	Caph	11	C	20
ל	Lamed	12	L	30
מ	Mem	13	M	40
נ	Noon	14	N	50
ס	Samech	15	S	60
ע	Ayin	16	ee/i	70
פ	Pei	17	P	80
צ	Tzaddi	18	Tz	90
ק	Koof	19	K	100
ר	Resh	20	R	200
ש ש	Sheen } Seen }	21	Sh	300
ת	Tav	22	T	400

ETZ Chaim
The Tree of Life

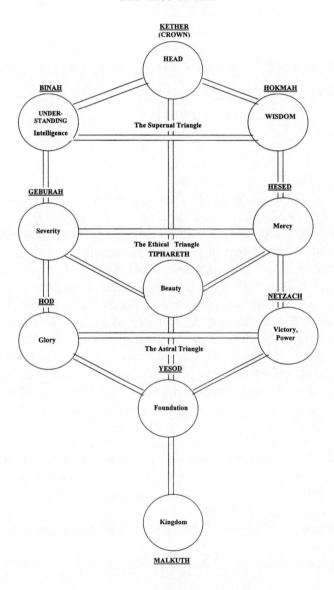

10

THOUGHTS AND CONSIDERATIONS OF THE KABBALA AND ITS UNWRITTEN CODE

The Kabbala claims to have originated before Abraham, its first supposed recipient. It does not belong to any specific tradition or religion, but was primarily regarded as the ancient, mystical wisdom of the Hebrews. Kabbala is basically a metaphysical system of religious theosophy relating to God and the Universe, a theory of emanation. It leads to a different interpretation of the Bible, especially the Pentateuch, from the normally accepted version. Claiming to be the oldest science in the world and the founder of astrology, it aims to clarify the true relationship between the Soul and Universal Man. Some of the earliest work is traced back to the Chaldees and Egypt, supposedly passed on by Abraham and later inherited by Joseph, with much of its truth revealed in his dreams. Inherited by Moses, it finally passed to David and Solomon.

The basis of Kabbala is Etz Chaim, the Tree of Life. God quickly banished Adam and Eve (mankind) from the Garden of Eden, after they had tasted the fruit of the Tree of Knowledge, seeking to limit the damage caused by their curiosity. Had they eaten of the Tree of Life, they would have gained immortality and He would never have been free of them.

Kabbalists see Universal Man represented on the Tree of Life, in all his physical and spiritual being. They claim that, as Kabbala means 'to receive', they became the rightful recipients of the inner Truth of the divine visitation, in the form of the ten manifestations called the Sephiroth. These were positioned on the Tree of Life in their interrelated Spheres, and were completely interlinked by 32 Paths of the Divine Emanations, all relating to mankind (see diagram on page 151).

Kabbala claims to derive its *modus vivendi* principally from the Book of the Law and the Prophets of the Old Testament; from the Talmud (knowledge), a collection of learned commentaries by the ancient, most learned Rabbis, who devoted their lives to biblical study and contemplation; and from their own, inspired Kabbalistic literature and oral inheritance, including the Zohar (Book of Splendour). The close relationship of Kabbala to the Scriptures is recognised immediately by the traditional ending of the Lord's Prayer: 'For thine is the Kingdom (Malkuth), the Power (Netzach) and the Glory (Hod)', derived from pure Kabbala.

The Greeks adopted the Kabbala, especially Pythagoras and Plato. When Kabbala re-emerged in the Middle Ages, it was said to be based on neo-Platonism, so close had the association become. Unfortunately the Catholic Church turned against Kabbala, wrongly scenting danger to its basic tenets. All possible traces of Kabbalistic records and literature were destroyed, especially its early relationship to astrology and the occult, on which much of its early theory and wisdom depended. Its knowledge and teachings could only be passed on orally thereafter, but nevertheless were carefully preserved until the early 12th century. Great new leaders then emerged, including Rabbi Isaac the Blind, called 'Father of Kabbala', who recreated interest in Kabbala throughout Europe. It was revised principally through astrology and alchemy, using the Tarot system of symbolism. Closely involved were the Signs of the Zodiac, the Planets and the Elements, 22 symbols related to Tarot trumps and the Hebrew alphabet of 22 letters (no vowels), indicating divine power.

The Catholic Church again weighed heavily against Kabbala and astrology, though many leading thinkers and philosophers remained supportive. So its influence waned in the late Middle Ages and was only revived in the 19th century. Modern Kabbala owes its resuscitation to some of the learned writers and philosophers who rediscovered it and renewed its study and teaching.

Discussion of Kabbala must needs commence with the description of the Tree of Life, which represents the Universe and its relationship with the Soul. The ten emanations on the Tree, the Sephiroth (Intelligences), are represented by ten Spheres, arranged on three vertical columns or pillars. At their head is the all-important KETHER, the Crown, the equilibrating Power. All Spheres are interrelated and interdependent, yet each is of a pure form. Man's physical body, emotions, mind and spirit, his whole being, is represented on the Tree by these manifestations of the Universe and Body and Soul of Man.

The Tree is divided into three Supernal Triangles. The first is called the Intellect, combining reason and liberty, and is the most important triad on which the others depend. It embraces the Crown at its head, with HOKMAH (Wisdom) on its right and BINAH (Intelligence and Understanding) heading the left column. These are the three Supernals from which comes Knowledge. Hokmah is also the Sphere of the Zodiac and Saturn, Father of the Gods, as in Tarot.

The Sephiroth are called the Spheres of the Planets. The right column under Hokmah is named Mercy. The left under Binah is Severity. The middle column under Kether is the column of

176

Equilibrium and Consciousness. This first supernal triangle represents the major concept of Head, Father and Mother. The second supernal triangle contains HESED, GEBURAH and TIPHARETH. HESED (Mercy and Love), on the right column, is associated with the Sphere of Planet Jupiter. GEBURAH (Justice, Strength and Fear) lies with the Sphere of Planet Mars, on the left column. TIPHARETH (Beauty) is aligned to the Sphere of the Sun and is the centre-point of our being, mediating between Creator and Creation. It represents mankind's supreme level, producing messiahs and world leaders. This triangle represents power, will and fatality. The third triangle contains NETZACH (Victory and Power) on the right column, assigned to Venus. It represents the material world, depending upon MALKUTH.

HOD (Glory and Intellect), represents conquest of mind over matter, active over passive, life over death. It is assigned to the Planet Mercury.

YESOD (Foundation), centre of the triangle, represents the Absolute in philosophy, the basis of all belief and truth.

MALKUTH (Kindom of the Earth) is not a constituent part of any triangle, and is assigned to the Moon. It represents the foundation rooted in the earth, the entire Creation and Universe. It also features in Tarot as Queen, 'Bride of God'.

These Sephiroth are all linked to the Tarot, each card of which bears a Kabbalistic meaning. Thus King, Queen, Knight, Page represent: the married pair, the youth, the child, the race.

Some Kabbalists contend that Moses received on Mount Sinai the keys to the Bible Code which guides the continued strength of its people, until they have accomplished their predestined mission for the world. They see God as exemplified to be possibly an hypothesis in this overall purpose, holding that Yahweh was but one of the family of spirits directed to their tasks and duties by the supreme Spirit, En Soph, who reigns overall, infinite, invisible. Hence Yahweh's assignment was the Creation of our World, with responsibility for all therein and, finally, the birth and guidance of mankind. This might explain the anthropomorphic image of Yahweh construed by J. The ten Sephiroth are manifestations of the spirits interlinked through Intelligence and Willpower (which must be carefully balanced with care and justice), leading to Grace and Perfection, with ultimate triumph of good over evil, with comfort for those who devote themselves to the service of others.

There is no death, no finality of destruction. Everything changes and becomes transformed on the journey through life. So man's physical body engenders the development of his mind, to become eventually transformed into pure Soul from the finite to the infinite. Thus destruction is overcome by love and faith, hope and trust in the highest Spirit as final resting place for the Soul, helped by dispensing with overmuch attention to human concerns, with self-sacrifice for the sake of others in greater need. The Universe has no bounds, no limits. It contains all creation, combining both evolution and devolution of all creatures save Man, who becomes the ultimate spiritual Soul. As one physical form ends and seemingly disappears, it is but to graduate to another, more perfect transmigration. Matter is in continuous movement. Hydrogen and oxygen atoms combine to produce water, which then produces clouds, rain, rivers and oceans. Mist and vapour are now drawn from the water, producing more clouds and rainfall. The constant repetition of this process produces more advanced living cells, until the formation finally of animal life, through the life-giving medium of water. Very slow, continuous development eventually produces Man, imbued with spirit to induce development of the human body and mind, and the Soul.

There are four external elements: Fire, Earth, Air and Water. Man and minerals combine in generation and development. The Soul moves from incarnation to reincarnation, from the term of life to death, to rebirth. The Astral Form, unseen, moves with the human, but is subject to magical manipulation. The Spirit Body is of higher state than the physical, remaining unseen until activated on the Astral Plane. Astral (Greek: related to a star) here relates to man, when able to leave his physical body and travel on the Astral Plane in his Astral Body which, though invisible, is just as real as the physical body it inhabits through its life.

There is nothing completely solid in the material world. Every atom, molecule, electron is in continuous, vibratory movement. The Astral has its own scenery, geography and surroundings just as the material world. The Astral Form is connected to its physical counterpart, by a tiny, slender thread of ethereal nature, capable of expansion and contraction, as in Ecclesiastes 12:6–7: 'Or ever the silver cord be loosed.... And the dust return to the earth as it was, and the spirit return unto God who gave it.' Generally the mind of the dying person sinks into the slumber of so-called death, and awakens only after a period of restful transforming tranquillity upon the Astral Plane, preparing for its next transformation.

Spirituality is the awareness of the divine spark within the Soul and the awakening into consciousness. Religion in the occult sense consists of observance of certain forms of worship, rites, ceremonies, accepted forms of theology and manifestations of religious emotions. We possess invisible powers of thought and intelligence. The mind has five facul-

179

ties: intellect, reason, perception, discrimination and the will. All Souls are allowed three rebirths. Only when the last Soul is reborn will the Messiah appear. Then all Souls will be reunited with En Soph, the Supreme Spirit.

The Divine Soul is on the highest level of the universe. It is the centre of good and noble aspirations – selfless, aspiring only to aid the weak and suffering. Pure Spirit is the Divine Self, never incarnated within any physical form, until the Seventh State of perfect manhood be attained. Man must work out his own salvation through his mastery of his own problems. According to Karma, the Soul can only reach its freedom when the full price has been paid, and all conditions met by nature's laws of truth and justice. Man must control his own development, from ignorance and primary animal instincts to a burgeoning of interest in higher evolution, thereby overcoming the problems of life, with struggles against oppressors and usurped authority. He should not accept other philosophies like the Buddhists, whose Karma taught those suffering under despotic rule to submit passively to the superior authority of church, and the tyranny of kings, emperors and dictators. By so submitting, they maintain, man is working off his previous bad Karma, so that he may emerge in higher form in reincarnation. Kabbala insists that the cruelty and wanton destruction of dictators should be courageously resisted, for the future development of mankind to the highest reaches of the paths leading to En Soph, the Divine Spirit.

Primitive man personified the seasons and stars after the animal spirits he worshipped. Clay tablets unearthed in profusion in Mesopotamia recorded astrological events as far back as 4000 BC. Astrologers from Sumeria, Assyria, Babylonia clearly predicted floods around 3500 BC. They were also the first known mathematicians and numerologists. They had, as yet, no alphabet of letters, but Sumerians were skilled in the use of code-like signs called cuneiform. They calculated the first calendar, were most inventive, established places of learning and constructed ziggurats, tower-like, to reach toward the heavens to study the stars, not yet possessing telescopes. Astrologers were esteemed as wise men with mystical and magical powers of the occult.

The Church, when formed, turned against astrology and the occult, fearing their hold on the people with their magical and prophetic powers. It feared and suppressed this quickening development of books, expanding men's minds and raising difficult questions and problems. But the progress of man's intelligence cannot be stopped whilst still in life, even with torture. The movements of stars and heavenly bodies continued to be observed, using the Zodiac to note the changing of the seasons and prediction of movements of sun, moon and planets, also their effect upon the earth, tides, animals and vegetation. Man has always questioned life and its meaning and relationship to himself, his reason for living and the essence of his being.

The Soul:	formless, intangible, an unseen presence, has affinity with the Divine Spirit.
The Senses:	are invisible, no shape or form: see, hear, smell, taste, feel.
The Form:	sound, colour, flavour, they relate to the brain, mind and physical body.
The Universe:	contains four essential essences: fire, water, earth and air.
Atoms:	are immortal, eternal, indestructible. Thus an organic whole may be destroyed, but not all of its parts. Death does not mean complete destruction. The body decays but the Soul endures. Just as fruit rots to allow its seed to be reborn, so decay is necessary

181

for new birth. Nature also has the problem of internal conflict, which may allow a false issue of evil with lies, murder, fraud, even religious falsification. Man is similarly subject to constant internal struggle of good against evil, self-interest against the common good, producing ill-will and ruthless rulers.

Letters:
Their use enables man to express himself and penetrate many hidden secrets. Hebrew letters were the first to be formed into an alphabet, primarily composed of three fundamental so-called mother letters: Aleph (A) air, Mem (M) water, Shin (Sh) fire, called AMSHEL. Then seven double letters which have two sounds, and 12 single letters. Fire (heat of summer season), relates to heaven, water (cold winter), relates to earth, and air (mild weather, spring and autumn) is the mediator. 3, 7 and 12 are the bricks which build the world: Fire, Water and Air, Man: Head, Body, Breast. In the Year: Heat, Cold, Wet. Man is 3, with head, heart and stomach. 7 are the openings of head, eyes, nostrils, mouth, ears. The Universe comprises 12 signs of Zodiac, 12 months of the year, the 12 capacities of sight, smell, speech, hearing, nutrition, generation, touch, locomotion, wrath, laughter, thought and sleep. Number 1 dominates 3, 3 governs 7, 7 is superior to 12, yet each part is inseparable from the whole, like the head from the body.

Over all letters and numbers hovers the Spirit: infinite, yet partaking in all.

There are 7 sacraments and 7 planets. 7 is the most welcome and fortunate number.

8 is the minority of the wise. 9 is the most sublime number.

4: the cardinal virtues, containing all the Mysteries of the Universe.

10: the 10 Commandments: the most perfect number, including: Unity and Zero, both symbols of nature and chaos. The Art of Prophecy: all Western peoples have their own forefathers stretching back to ancient Eastern civilisations. Prophecy originated in Mesopotamia with the Sumerians and Hebrews, especially influenced by astrology, provoking immediate reactions of fear and urgent desire to escape the consequences. Man lives among predictions and even intuition. Some of the great prophets of history (non-biblical) were:

Zoroaster	in the 7th century BC. Inventor of magic.
Roger Bacon:	Franciscan Friar (1214–94), student of experimental science and optics, produced his *opus majus* work based on Aristotle's philosophy. Foresaw machines of navigation, large ships moving without oars, carriages travelling at speed without horses. Flying machines with wings flapping like birds. Like Rabbi Moses Maimonides, Bacon believed the Holy Writ was the basic source of Astrology, as claimed by Kabbala.
Agrippa:	Renaissance man immersed in supernatural and occult, wrote *Occult Philosophy*, believing men could work miracles by power of their wisdom.
Nostradamus	(Michel de Notre-Dame) 1503–66: greatest of all seers and astrologers. Wrote 'Centu-

ries' 1555, containing his prophecies; physician, scientist and prophet.

Astrology was practised by Sumerians, Chaldeans, Egyptians, Hebrews, Babylonians, Assyrians, Greeks and Persians, who were also skilled mathematicians without the use of telescopes or mechanical instruments. They were convinced that nothing happened by chance. Everything depended on whether the stars were favourable or unfavourable. The planets were the most important heavenly bodies as they manifested power, moving on their individual paths, differing from the fixed stars.

There were two great laws by which the planets affected human organism: harmony and discord. Nature divided the Zodiac into equal arcs of light and darkness, winter and summer, Northern and Southern Signs. The 12 signs of the Zodiac corresponded to the 12 sons of Jacob.

The Sun: was worshipped by all mankind, as the central spiritual source of life – the creative power and the healer.

The Moon: Luna – the universal mother. Hers was the secret of movement of tides, mysteries of gestation, and alternating periods of fruitfulness and sterility.

Astrology: is the science of the stars. Each of the nine planets within our Universe has a special influence on all things on earth. There are only nine stars within our solar system: Sun, Moon, Mercury, Venus, Mars, Saturn, Uranus, Jupiter, Neptune, all revolving continuously around the earth at different rates of speed. They travel through space by the Zodiac which has 12 sections, named

Signs: Aries, Taurus, Gemini, Cancer, Leo, Virgo, Libra, Scorpio, Sagittarius, Capricorn, Aquarius and Pisces.

Ephemens: is the astronomical almanac for the year, giving exact position of each planet in degrees, minutes and seconds for every day and month.

The Science of Numerology: all letters of the alphabet have numerical equations. Therefore all combinations of letters in names contain a certain numerical value. Nature in its most primitive form responds to numbers (as with prisms of ice and snowflakes), movement of heavenly bodies and the recurrence of the seasons. The Kabbala discerns hidden meanings in biblical letters and words. By forming new words, anagrams and numbers, new formations of the first letters of words and abbreviations are produced. The Roman method of *notaricun* made abbreviations, using initials of words joined together so that the first and last became new words. The Romans were the first to introduce shorthand.

Temurah: substitutes, transposes and permutes letters of words – thus anagrams with hidden meaning. For example, the first-ever Hebrew substitution code was by simply reversing the alphabet, whether wholly (as later followed by the Romans in their Caesar code) or partially e.g. A > Z, B > Y etc. Kabbalists would thus discover hidden meanings like cryptologists – one word would produce another. The fundamental number is 10 – composed of 1, 'One is the spirit of the living God', and 0, which is the extent of the finite and explains dreams.

The Tarot: a complete set of 78 symbolical picture cards, supposedly of Egyptian, Celtic or Indian origin. First invented in Italy in the 14th century as a pack of playing cards of divine origin. The Tarot is closely associated with the Kabbala and uses its Tree of Life. Kabbala deems Tarot cards to be the key to the esoteric tradition of the Jews, as stated by Eliphas Levi (1855) as 'the primitive source of divine and human tradition'. Tarot's theories devolve upon nature and infinite truths, claiming that everything that obtains in the universe is caused by pre-established laws.

The Tarot figures are archetypes, yet claim to release one's own psychic powers and abilities to divine images and experiences. There are 22 pictorial cards, called Trumps, with symbolic figures such as a hanged man, hermit, pope, king and queen, jester, knave and fool. There are four suits each of 14 cards: Wands, Cups, Swords and Pentacles, equalling Diamonds, Spades, Clubs and Hearts. One card is a 'wild card'. The 22 Trump cards match the Hebrew alphabet.

It has been claimed that the doctrine of En Soph (Supreme Spirit) and the Sephiroth was not known before the 13th century. A certain Rabbi Solomon ben Abraham (most significant name) frankly declared his disbelief. He declared that this doctrine was neither to be found in the Law, the Prophets or Hagiographs, but simply depended on unknown, scarcely recognisable signs. However, a 'school' of Kabbala is still active in Israel and America.

I must express my gratitude for the information I have been able to cull from some of the most learned writers on Kabbala, who have shed light on this engrossing subject, of which my knowledge proved to be so much less than their authoritative depth. I am most grateful to Zolar for his most fascinating book: *The Encyclopaedia of Ancient and Forbidden Knowledge*; Dion Fortune: *The Mystical Qaballah*; Charles Poncé: *Kabbalah*; Carlo Saures: *The Cipher of Genesis*; Christian D. Ginsburg: *The Essenes* and *The Kabbalah* – two excellent essays; and Leo Schaya: *The Universal Meaning of*

Kaballah. They were so convincing, they almost converted me, a proof-seeking cryptologist. I hope they will forgive my efforts to probe into and extract gems from their work, as a fellow scribe of lesser knowledge and significance.

11

RELIGIOUS DEVELOPMENT

Primitive man, the hunter and gatherer, had simple basic needs – food and protection. He soon realised his dependency upon the elements. Sun, moon, water, fire, were essential to his well-being and sustenance. Gradually their significance grew, as superior beings to whom he owed deference, respect and fear, as when light suddenly became mysterious, threatening dark. So fire was essential for light, warmth, cooking and security against prowlers. From such dependence grew his primitive form of worship.

Family protection activated construction of stockades, with the co-operation of neighbours and agreement on general behaviour and respect for each other's property and privacy. Groups became communities, requiring firm rules of conduct, with respect not only for each individual but also for the elements. Discovery of the germination of seeds and vegetation, and domestication of animals, aided progress from signs and pictograms to words and the first forms of language, some 35,000 years ago, according to Richard Leakey. Everything other than mankind remained fixed at some level of evolution, progressing no further. But mankind continued to develop mentally and physically into and beyond the first advent of civilisation.

The beginning of language brought the first rudiments of

religion and personification of gods of nature. These were carved out of wood, clay and stone in human form. Hence they were given human characteristics and emotions but also supernatural and magical powers. Gods developed their own individual personalities and spiritual power, growing in importance and value. They responded to worship by ever-increasing human concepts of attention, sacrifice and gifts. Their importance grew with fanciful tales of their powers and exploits, passed on orally until set in place with the invention of writing. Principal gods now made increasing demands on their imaginative worshippers, who responded with human and animal sacrifices, celebration of their festive seasons, such as harvest, and the building of altars, shrines and finally temples to house their particular gods.

The great mix of nomadic communities in the ancient Near and Middle East were known as Hibaru. From them evolved a close-knit group called Ibri ('Apiru' by Egypt), who eventually became the Hebrews. At first they retained these inherited customs and shared the same gods, sagas and folklore. They gradually separated from the main body who shared the same Semitic background and themselves gradually split off into their own generic groups, becoming Akkadians, Assyrians, Babylonians, Hittites. All then sought to expand by taking over each other's cities and areas by force, especially the rich land known as the Fertile Crescent, around the great rivers of Tigris and Euphrates, later called Mesopotamia (between two rivers).

This drive for expansion continued through all following centuries in ever increasing brutality. Even in our present time we have witnessed this evil thrust by modern advanced terrorism, twisting our great scientific and technical discoveries for the benefit of mankind, to their evil intent of striking at the heart of Western culture and religious faith, especially aimed at Christianity born of Judaism.

Evil has many heads which, despite all our efforts, seem to defy our peace-loving civilisation with instantaneous new growth. Just as in those distant biblical times, the struggle will be long and wearying and costly in precious lives until victory and lasting peace are finally won.

It was with these ancient Hebrews that our religion began. As shown, the first eleven chapters of Genesis owe their mythological beginning mainly to the folklore and epic legends of those early gods they inherited and still worshipped. Archaeologist George Smith unearthed thousands of clay tablets revealing the history and first religions of those countries and people. From the Sumerians, who apparently arrived from the Indus valley about 5000 BC, to the Phoenicians, who came from the sea about 1100 BC, came a host of colourful information revealing their customs, inventions and general progress, with various forms of worship.

About 3500 BC those interesting, cultured and early civilised Sumerians, who had originally constructed dwellings of mud mixed with straw, now progressed to build stone houses, invented the first ploughs to develop farming, the first wheels of solid wood, with rough carts (from which came the chariots) and above all, the first form of writing in cuneiform script of hundreds of signs and symbols. From this flowed book-keeping, accounts, music and art to decorate their first temples. They constructed tall buildings, schools and pyramid-style ziggurats reaching towards the heavens and the stars they sought to study by the beginning of astrology. They worshipped all the ancient gods but mainly Nanna, the moon goddess.

Their *Epic of Creation* and the Babylonians' *Epic of Gilgamesh*, with similar tales from other countries, provide all the evidence to prove that the original author of the Pentateuch drew much of his material from those earlier sources. Especially his account of the Creation and birth of Adam, from the Beginning to Babel in chapter 11 of Genesis. His principal character Yahweh, his anthropomorphic One God, above all other gods, seems to relate to Marduk, King of all the gods in Gilgamesh. All with strong human characteristics and emotions, reacting like men to most situations, but heartless and insensitive to human feelings. Yet supernatural beings with magical powers, making arbitrary demands on their followers, who fear dire punishment, such as ruination of their crops and causing blight and sickness if neglected. These foreshadow the Yahweh of Genesis. How would he be regarded in our time? Maybe we need him on our side right now, to mete out his harshest punishment on modern terrorists who seek to murder men, women and children in massive numbers, usurping his authority The Yahweh of the Old Testament would not hesitate to eliminate such evil-doers, by plague, fire or flood, instantaneously.

Yahweh towers above them all from the outset. He is in close contact with his creatures from the moment of their inception: 'in our image after our likeness'. But there it apparently ceases. Ever-watchful, ready to pounce on the slightest misdemeanour or divergence from the narrow path he lays down for them, his punishments are immediate, harsh, unforgiving and penetrating, even to death, from individuals to mass numbers. No mercy, no forgiving the repentant sinner. From kings to slaves, all are meted out the most severe punishments for any crime, especially that of returning to worship other gods and graven images. Such a hard, merciless One God, who is jealous of any competition from other gods, would provoke fear rather than loving obedience and worship. 'The fear of

191

the Lord', in his case, brought not wisdom but complete obedience to avoid harsh punishment, disease or death. How would he be regarded in our time?

Yet there were some who cheerfully followed his edicts and fulfilled his demands to the best of their ability. For this was no easy religion to follow, as portrayed by J, the original author, whose work still obtains in its greater part in all Bibles. After the mythological first eleven chapters of Genesis, the real history of Judaism then begins with the first great monotheist of the Bible, the Patriarch Abraham. His name is fully respected alike in all three major religions of Judaism, Christianity and Islam, for he is 'Father of All Nations'. About 2200 BC he first smashes all the idols his father Terah makes as his trade, and sets forth to Haran with his wife Sarai, obeying Yahweh's call to leave Ur of the Chaldees, land of the magicians. Only just in time, for the city was ruined and burnt to the ground soon after their departure.

Now begins the story of the history and religion of our ancestors, at Yahweh's instructions: first to go to Canaan, to be shown the land his descendants must battle their way through to reach their 'Promised Land', of which we are to hear so much and so often. Thence to Egypt to avoid the famine, then to resume their wandering under guidance, until the amusing scene of Sarai's mockery of Yahweh on hearing his promise to Abraham, aged 100, of a son for her, now barren at 90. Yahweh, annoyed at being laughed at by Sarai, said: 'Nay; but thou didst laugh. Is any thing too hard for Yahweh?' (Genesis 18:14–15) He demands total belief and obedience.

Yahweh's plans are not revealed until after the birth of Isaac (means: to laugh), and a further example of Yahweh's urge for wholesale destruction at Sodom and Gomorrah. This is but the lead-in to the birth of Jacob (the sideshow of the tussle of

192

the twins has its counterpart in Gilgamesh), who, after maturing with his entertaining love story, is due to become Israel (soldier of God). That marks the cornerstone of the history and religious growth of the Israelites, to be beaten into shape with their 400-year long experiences in Egypt, from welcome heroes to brutally beaten slaves (Apiru).

Some maintain that the true history and religion of the Jews really began with the Exodus from Egypt, and the toughening experience of those 40 years of hungry and thirsty wandering in the desert wasteland (similar to the toughening training of modern soldiers). It was the mysterious character called Moses who parented them during these years of hardening. He it was who really taught them their monotheistic religion, with exact details of all that it entailed. For the first time they learnt their true religion with all its laws and disciplines, its code of conduct with detailed instructions from the form of their prayers to what was permitted as fit to eat and drink, and what needed to be avoided in that desert heat and conditions. These dietary laws kept them free from disease and sickness prevalent in all that region. There is no mention of sickness or ill-health throughout Exodus.

On reaching their 'Promised Land', become Israel (*anent* Palestine), the history of this battle-hardened nation of warriors now takes firm hold. They have their religion and their One God, fought for grimly through bitter struggles and combats, never revealed in advance by Yahweh, in case they might cut and run, as they sought to do on hearing the exaggerated reports of the spies sent forth by Abraham – eventually proven not so wrong after all. With their precious Ark of the Covenant proudly carried before them in battle, they are now true believers, with their battle-cry 'Hear, O Israel, the Lord, our God, the Lord is One'... Yet they still held fast to their ancient gods and carved images (though the making of statues was forbidden), now apparently accepted by Yahweh, who demands to be set above and 'before all other gods' in his Commandments. Moses, priests, judges and kings all accept the continued presence of Baal and Astarte and still turn to them for silent comfort away from the fierce wrath of militant Yahweh.

What then is this religion which holds them so firmly, despite their anthropomorphic, ever-demanding, punishing Creator? Moses' Ten Commandments and rules of prayer and conduct were established after Exodus from Egypt about 1200 BC, never to be lost by whatever suffering will undoubtedly accrue. Despite all their hardships, brutal, harsh and unjust treatment throughout the ages, that heartfelt cry: 'Hear, O Israel, the Lord our God, the Lord is One' rings undaunted through the centuries of exile, and still remains their watchword. Their faith is constant, enduring and indefinable, and despite torture, massacre, assassination, holocaust, remains indestructible. We have much to learn from their indomitable faith and will. The brave reaction of Americans to the present terrorists' (Arabs and Muslims) massacre and slaughter of the innocents in the New York World Trade Center, revealed that same independence of faith and courage of their ancestors.

History proves that there can be no lasting victory for tyranny and dictatorships as imposed in Africa, Burma, Iraq, Iran, Syria, Palestine and the Taliban with Osama bin Laden in Afghanistan. All those tyrannical empires of the past have crumbled to dust. Their dictators imposed their will on the suffering people only till they met their death, usually by assassination. We have had to suffer two world wars, losing thereby millions of our loyal youth on which our future depended, imposed for no valid reason by a German Kaiser and a Nazi German dictator.

But other wars and massacres have continued throughout the past and present centuries, compelling our Western peace-seeking nations to take up arms in support of tortured and suffering people. Millions of innnocent lives deprived in the name of religion, as in the Nazi holocaust, cry out to us for retribution. At last we now realise that the struggle against terrorism in all its forms must continue, however long it may take, until its very roots are eradicated.

True, the early portrayal of Yahweh has been changed after those early years of the Beginning and development of BC, to the more peaceful, loving, merciful, forgiving Adonai and Jehovah of AD. But who can explain the mystery of their constancy through all the changes and suffering of those following terrible centuries, when other peoples were so easily converted? It is also difficult to explain how Christianity managed to survive (still maintaining its Hebrew roots) and continue to develop. The mysterious conversion of Paul from his erstwhile stoning of the Jews and murder of Stephen, could not be accepted or believed by most of the disciples. Their rejection drove him to become missionary to the Gentiles, which he accomplished with great energy and success. His teaching was basically Judaism founded on the Old Testament.

Dr Leo Baeck described the Hebrew religion as: 'The idea and challenge of the One that alone is needful, the Good, the Right, the One God beside whom there is none else. It means the totality of man. With his whole heart and soul, man is to serve the One God and Him only. There is only one reality, the One God, his commandment and the doing of it.' That is the true voice of monotheism, with its basically plain, ungarnished faith. No half-measures, no other possibility or subdivision, questioning or deviation from that solid belief. Even though nowadays, as in the Christian and Islamic faiths, so many react against the pageantry or endless repetitive set forms of services and prayers, and the trappings and overabundance of outworn side issues (such as styles of dress, wearing of hats or outward appearance or stylised manner of prayer)... that basic concept taught from earliest childhood remains untarnished, but quiescent.

The basic foundation of Christian theology and the precepts of Christian conduct and character, likewise of Islam, with Mohammed, their great and abiding Prophet, demanded full obedience to the commands and will of Allah like the Hebrew Prophets to Yahweh. It has come a long way from the primitive beliefs of all our ancient ancestors, worshipping gods of nature, then the polytheistic culture of the Sumerians or the early polydaemonistic *cultus* of the first Hebrews. There is no indication of how and when the Hebrew religion became monotheistic, except that it is first evidenced with Abraham, about 2200 BC, to be finally confirmed by Moses some 1000 years later. Even then, the Commandments revealed the continued acceptance of their earlier gods: 'Thou shalt have no other gods before Me.' It was the *nabi*, the great Prophets of the Bronze Age, seeking no material gains, solely the truth, who really proclaimed the Sole God, with new-found strength, mercy and goodness, for the first time. Especially Jeremiah who risked his own death in stating the truth and castigating the selfish, greedy, dishonest priests, busily pursuing their own ends. Through the Prophets the other gods were cast aside, and Baal and his ilk done away with, though even today some still worship 'graven images' and possess their own particular idols, especially, for example, the prevalent god Mammon.

The Christian Church first believed it was the spiritual development of Judaism. It adopted the Old Testament as its basic Scriptures and, after the first Council of Jerusalem, abandoned both the rite of circumcision and kosher food (according to

Jewish law). Baptism, however, was an old Jewish custom, adopted by Christ as initiation rite (c.f. John the Baptist). Communion developed out of the Jewish religious meal held on the eve of Sabbath. It too was taken over by the Christian Church. Likewise the old Hebrew belief that only by doing justice, loving mercy and walking humbly with God can one draw near to Him.

Over the centuries Judaism and Islam have held fast to their One God or Allah, whilst Christianity has split between warring factions and different shades of Catholicism, Protestantism and manifold breakaway groups and versions and -isms. For Judaism and Islam the word became the Book, Bible or Koran. For Christians the 'word became flesh'. A common, accepted world faith now would be the final peak of achievement for all three closely related versions.

Continuing scientific discoveries tend to challenge previous concepts of our inheritance and culture, way of life, habits, traditions, morals, ethics. What changes will the next century bring to our views on education, religion and the churches? Many are still prepared to accept undemanding religious precepts, undisturbing to their present comfortable situation. But there has never been in world history such extreme, brutal violence as in this century. Two major wars and maniacal madness of twisted minds caused loss, torture and bestial destruction, and wastage of millions of innocent lives, and the disappearance of more empires than ever previously recorded or threatened. Old conflicts have been prolonged or renewed in many parts of the world, continuing, even now, further senseless destruction. We produce and priests even bless more and more deadly weapons, whilst at the same time continuing to pray for peace and tolerance. Science brings new weapons of mass destruction and chemical agony, as well as new benefits and alleviation. It seems almost a mockery. Which to

197

choose – brutal death or longer, healthier life? Cynics might say that one helps to pay for the other. Do we need a new Churchillian figure to lead the battle against all wars, or a new Prophet to lead us to an all-embracing worldwide religion without any internecine problems?

The aftereffects of war seem to imbue us with a renewed drive towards material benefits and comforts as compensation. Our world is perilously unbalanced and our inner state disordered. There are growing alliances of humane care and activity (of which the British seem outstandingly inspired), directed to generous charitable actions. Yet the growing desperation caused by extremists and fanatics of evil intent, who still inspire fear and suffering of the innocent, unprotected and dispossessed, demands concerted action. We exclaim with horror at recurring scenes of bestiality and cold-blooded murder of women and children, in the name or excuse of so-called religion, without feeling compulsion to take or compel action on national and international scale to stop, prevent and dismantle such inhuman activities. In some ways we are like lemmings moving irresistibly towards our final destruction and obliteration, without the willpower to stop this involuntary death-wish and change the deadly course of modern history to the better promotion of worldwide peaceful co-operation to bring spiritual as well as material benefits to all mankind.

It now lies within people's power to compel their leaders, statesmen, governments to come together urgently, without the usual bickering and procrastination (at which all seem so well practised), in joint, positive determination and compulsion to take immediate action to stop and remove this powerful evil element within every country, area or district. Especially the extremists and fanatics, whether in Algeria, Sudan, Egypt, Palestine, Lebanon, Syria, Iraq, Iran, Pakistan, India, Afghanistan, Arab States – the list seems endless – and

198

it is a cancerous growth which seems to extend rapidly, causing horrific agony, death and destruction. No country can unequivocally state that it is entirely free of this evil: Britain, Ireland, France, Germany, Ceylon, America, it is everywhere to be found, all seemingly well supplied with guns, bombs, mines and other murderous weapons, including chemicals, which must be removed from those who seem to take diabolical, inhuman pleasure in the maiming or destruction of their fellow human beings, with some fanatical belief in some extreme faith or branch of religion twisted to suit their own devices, like the misshapen Nazi cross, the Hakenkreuz.

This brief tracing of the birth and development of religion through world history leaves us with the bitter realisation that religion *per se* has not brought mankind the peaceful, tolerant faith and belief it should have achieved. Over all these countless years, peace and serenity and love of our fellow creatures has never succeeded in going hand-in-hand with the prayers and practices of any man-made religion with whatever gods have been created and worshipped. So where do we turn for relief? Certainly not to religious leaders to stop all wars and evil deeds and inhumanity. They would assume their self-created panoply, with prayers for wishful, spiritual aid and solace in our distress, but never any vigorous, concerted, co-operative, definite action to stop mankind's unceasing hurt, wounding, murder and suffering. The powerful continue, as ever, to oppress and plunder and hurt the weak and unprotected, the wealthy preying on the poor, extracting their very marrow and sinews.

Hope can only come from an exceptionally strong saviour from the people. Certainly not to be expected from governments, as we have known and experienced them throughout our world history. Could we possibly hope for a concerted movement from the general population led by men and women of courage and spirit – not for any bloody revolution like the ill-fated French or Russian, but for a united co-operation to assert their full rights, as once averred by world figures like Benjamin Franklin, Gandhi and Adam Smith, who, despite their own imperfections, were inspired by the urge towards the freedom and rights to life, liberty and sustenance of all human beings. There are no signs that this could come from a Supreme Spirit, who so far has presided over the mortal sufferings of humanity without producing the expected merciful relief, and complete unison and co-operation of all mankind. Or must one give up all such hopes and just pursue our course as lemmings irresistibly drawn to our final, irrevocable self-immolation and destruction? Or will the augured catastrophic collision put a shattered end to all our speculations?

Religion is a man-made institution. It is surely time for mankind to realise and examine its deficiencies and failures, and seek to find better and more lasting solutions to the urgent need of stopping all warfare and senseless, criminal maiming and murder of innocent people. There has to be a better way forward to ensure the peaceful tolerance, understanding and full co-operation of all nations, all peoples, all races, all levels to feed and minister to the needs of all humanity. If not a messiah who would gather up all the ends, then perhaps in the meantime we should hope and pray for a saviour, a David, champion of the people, to come forth. There can be no doubt that millions would leave the pedestrian ranks of politics and the unproductive variety of religions, and devote complete support to what might well become the united human-created religion of the future, for the benefit of all mankind. More to the point, the redevelopment, expansion and full strengthening of the United Nations, would become the real guarantee of the safe-keeping of world peace.

200

Yet good does eventually surface from the holocaust of evil of this most destructive century. Especially in Britain where evidence of its people's natural gift of tolerance and patient endurance (whilst trying to see another's point of view and rendering assistance where possible) shines through the murk elsewhere existing, of people who turn away to avoid awareness of others' problems and suffering.

It is no longer the case of only the poor helping the poor. In country areas, the erstwhile differences of artificial class distinction are gradually moving away, replaced by the general desire of the vast majority to give sympathetic understanding and assistance to fellow creatures and sufferers, especially the increasing numbers of elderly and disabled. Groups of voluntary helpers have grown amazingly strong and prolific in this decade. Rich and poor, professional and manual workers, all seem no longer imbued with the erstwhile incessant clamour for wealth and material benefits. The now all-too-frequent redundancies, have produced a general feeling of awareness of the really valid qualities of life. Giving one's services freely and positively wherever possible, seems to release the fount of human kindness and generosity of spirit, which threatened to dry up in the materialistic situation of the post-war years. 'Job satisfaction' and 'social companionship' have become more important for many than the restless surge after higher rewards, now recognised as unsustainable.

We are constantly aware of the problems, domestic worries, divorces and misery of so many who seem to acquire wealth too quickly and easily, then dispense and waste it almost as quickly on momentary excitement, which never guarantees long-term happiness. That spirit of true happiness and. contentment is to be found in partners sharing the problems of working for their living – whilst being aware of the. problems of others in worse condition. Equal sharing of

201

family love and responsiblilty is the obvious solution of much present discontent.

Contentment now seems to lie more in the ability to provide sufficient for the family, with regular saving towards adequate pension on retirement, to cater for future elderly needs. The fact that we are now living to a much older age than our grandparents is due not only to healthier living, but more to the acceptance of life as it progresses, meeting all problems with firm fortitude. We are sustained by the boon of the free National Health Service, though its costs are rising too fast for containment, demanding careful reshaping, including the tremendous cost of all the meals so carefully prepared and served daily.

This is all part of the new realism of religion. People are now finding their own way to serious thought and consideration of life's meaning, after the suffering of two World Wars — soon after the Boer War, followed by the Falklands, then the Gulf War and all too many major and minor conflicts throughout the world. The United Nations organisation is gradually succeeding in its concerted efforts to bring about peaceful settlements everywhere, in place of bloodshed, brutal murders, destruction of homes and cities.

Still dimly, but ever more surely, we can envisage a not-too-distant future when our children will be able to mature without any impending threat of war hanging over them. Peace is becoming the watchword, well proven in settled value in the past 50 years in Western Europe. It is surely well within the good faith of the major countries, including America, Russia (still seeking a true democratic base), China, Japan, to weave together a peaceful pact or settlement, leading to genuine friendship in the Middle East, between the Arab States within themselves and with Israel. It is to be devoutly hoped that such a state of lasting peace (needing a modern miracle) between all the Arab States, with Egypt, Jordan, Sudan, Iraq, Iran, Syria, Libya and Lebanon, the Palestinians and Israel, would bring prosperity and neighbourly co-opera- tion to the benefit of all their suffering peoples. It needs another Abraham, Father of All Nations, to bring them all together in the knowledge and appreciation that they are all equally his children.

There are so many troubled areas everywhere, including erstwhile Yugoslavia, still recovering from its self-inflicted wounds, Algeria, Sri Lanka, Korea, Afghanistan, Burma, Ireland, the list seems endless. The entire world is now becoming aware through the modern channels of immediate communication, that it is in urgent need of self healing before it brings upon itself the final all-shattering nuclear holocaust, eliminating everybody and everything produced by mankind, in total eclipse. Life, being, faith, religious belief, like time, would no longer be relevant.

So, for the sake of our children and future generations, let us cry together with one voice: Stop — this madness of self- destruction must now cease, and give way to immediate sober consideration of the necessity of all-embracing world peace. Concerted action to turn wrong into right, evil into good and neglect into care of all the suffering and needy. Only thus may faith and a really meaningful religion be measured.

Terrorism

Terrorism has always existed. Evil so often triumphs, with mankind's urgent desire for violence, brutality and destruction overriding better instincts. Originally arising from envy and greed, to be later inflamed by religious fanaticism, accompanying torture (as with the Inquisition) as means of conversion, with death as alternative.

We trace the dawn of our civilisation to the Sumerians, who invented the wheel, the first alphabetic signs (on clay tablets) and numbers, kept accounts and even opened schools. They became so contentedly prosperous as to incur the unprincipled jealous wrath of uncivilised neighbouring tribes including Assyrians (later Iraqis) who destroyed and gutted them and their creations.

The Egyptian Pharaohs first welcomed the industrious Hebrews, then became jealous of their waxing strength, skills in agriculture, building and development, then enslaved and terrorised them, finally reducing their growth drastically by murdering all their first-born sons. A destructive measure visited by the militant God of the Hebrews on the Egyptians in their turn for refusing to let his people go. He then destroyed Pharaoh's army and charioteers by drowning them in the Nile when pursuing the Hebrews.

That same militant God of the Old Testament proceeded to drown the whole world in extensive floods, later destroying Sodom and Gomorrah by fire, after terrorising the Israelites for 40 years in the wilderness with plagues and drastic punishment (swallowed up by the earth), and finally breaking his promise to take them to the Promised Land by killing them off, with Moses their gallant heroic leader, within sight of that land 'flowing with milk and honey'.

Terrorism has stalked the earth ever since. Its worst forms since biblical times have proved to be based on religious fanaticism, from the Catholic Inquisition to the most extreme fanatics of the Arabs and Muslims penetrating every continent

204

and country. Not content with overrunning almost the whole of the Near East.

Before the death of Muhammad in 632, all Arabia had accepted Islam. By 711, Islam had spread from Spain to India, terrorising whole populations into conversion of death. Their armies penetrated the Persian and Byzantine empires, then Egypt. Their penetration now covers the whole of the broad mass from Kazakhstan and Uzbekistan through Afghanistan, Pakistan, part of India and Bangladesh, Iran and Iraq, Syria and Turkey to Jordan and Saudi Arabia and Yemen. Then through the desert to Egypt, Eritrea, Sudan to Libya, Algeria, Senegal to the Ivory Coast. Still they grow from Nigeria, Ethiopia, Somalia, Mozambique and Madagascar. Then a leap across to Indonesia.

Their zealots are totally determined to spread even further, and already have ever-growing numbers throughout Europe, especially Britain and overseas to the USA and Canada. But their determination in total conversion and elimination of all other religions, faiths and beliefs, especially Christian and Jewish, their major targets.

These fanatical extremists are prepared to use any weapons, be they explosives, technical or nuclear, poisonous gases or chemicals. Their object is to wipe out very large quantities of the Western population, to strike them with fear, dread and despair. Then they offer their only peaceful solution: join them and submit to their bin Laden-type regime. No matter that these fanatics no longer bother with the true teaching of the Koran and its peaceful exhortations on preservation and care of life. Their new teaching of total sacrifice of one's life in pursuit of their aims of subjection and conquest, to explode oneself into fragments to defeat and conquer Jews and Christians and all other enemies of bin Laden, in order to reach the welcoming arms of Allah to receive due reward, seems to attract many lacking in intelligence or common sense.

I suspect they are loaded to the gunnels with drugs (and maybe the forbidden alcohol) to produce the required state of ecstasy (and maybe hypnotism), for I do not believe it possible for any normal person to commit suicide by blowing himself to pieces.

Islam and the Koran

Islam means 'submission' and a Muslim submits to the will of Allah. Their prophet Muhammad, the founder of Islam, was born in 570 AD in Mecca on the Arabian peninsula, the present Saudi Arabia. Orphaned at an early age, he was brought up by his uncle Abu Talib to become a merchant.

In fact he was a good merchant, of such undisputed honesty that he became known as 'Al-Ameen' – 'The Trustworthy'. He married Khadijah, a wealthy widow, who had employed him.

Of spiritual nature, he often retreated to a lonely cave in the mountain above Mecca, for meditation. It was there that he had a visitation from the Archangel Gabriel, who informed him that he had been chosen to be the prophet of Allah, the one true God. Terrified at this astounding revelation, he confided the awesome news to his wife, who comforted him and became his first convert to Islam.

Then aged about 42, Muhammad continued to receive revelations from Gabriel, which were duly recorded by his scribes as he began to recite as commanded: 'Recite in the name of your Lord, who created man from a blood-clot'. For the next 23 years his revelations from Gabriel were recorded and collected as the Koran.

The Koran has become the great prayer source to be constantly repeated and memorised. Islam is now the world's second largest religion, with over one billion Muslims, dominating some 16 countries. From Africa to Indonesia, Kazakhstan to Bangladesh, Morocco to Somalia, Turkey to the Gambia, also penetrating most others, including America, Britain and other European countries.

Muslims submit unquestioningly to the will of Allah. They accept the Koran as the word of Allah recorded by their supreme prophet Muhammad. His life was seen as a preparation for the next higher stage under Allah. But his early years were most difficult. He had to overcome strong attacks by Quraish tribes of Mecca, by marching on Mecca with an army of 10,000 Muslims. Seizing the city, Mecca was adopted as the spiritual centre of the Islamic world. In 632 Muhammad made his final pilgrimage there, leading about 150,000 men and women, who were accepted as of equal status. He then died, aged 62.

The true Islam is non-aggressive. The Koran preaches tolerance of other races and religions, especially Christians and Jews. Muhammad said: 'The true Muslim is the one who hurts no one by word or deed.' War is permitted only in self-defence to protect civilians. Though they set out in the 7th century to conquer the Middle East, central Asia, India, Spain, etc, they were enlightened warriors and conquerors, tolerant of religious minorities; unlike the Crusaders, who engaged in wholesale slaughter.

By the end of the 9th century the rules of the Koran, as laid down by Muhammad, had been codified into the Shari'ah.

207

Jihad, meaning 'to struggle in the path of God', meant a moral struggle against temptation with good works. Extreme Muslims seek to give it a different meaning of violence — which was never intended, nor to be found in the Koran.

Thus the Wahhabi sect, founded in the 18th century by Muhammad ibn Abd al-Wahhab, is extremist. They permit no music whatsoever, except the drums; no drinking, no ornaments, no idolatry, no self-exposure by women, who must appear always completely covered by burqas head to toe and are not allowed to work outside the home. Exiled for his extremism, he moved north to Nejd, where he converted the Saudi tribe, who then waged war on their neighbours until the establishment of Saudi Arabia in 1932.

Terrorists are produced by the Wahhabi sect, who sent suicide bombers to Israel and Egypt and elsewhere. Osama bin Laden is a Wahhabi. He swore to destroy the royal Saudis for allowing American troops on its soil during Desert Storm and subsequently. He forbids the presence of Jews or Christians on the Arabian peninsula. Exiled, he fled to the Talibans in Afghanistan, themselves Wahhabis. They are detested by the majority of traditional Muslims who follow the Koran's teaching of tolerance, laying down rules of behaviour codified legally in the Shari'ah.

Muhammad defines five pillars as foundations of Islam:

1. Shahadatayn, called 'Two Testimonies' of creed, affirming 'there is no god but God', similar to the Old Testament's 'Hear, O Israel, the Lord thy God is One'. Also, like Moses, Muhammad is chosen as his prophet to explain Allah's will to his people. After Muhammad, they expect the Second Coming of a prophet like Jesus Christ. Like Jews and Christians they worship the same God and accept

Abraham as their forebear and father of Ishmael, Father of Faith in One God — the first monotheist.
2. The duty to pray five times daily, at dawn, midday, mid-afternoon, sunset and nightfall. No sacrament, needing no priest. Every believer faces Allah alone.
3. Zakat is the regular giving of alms, with a minimum of one-fortieth of one's income offered annually to charity.
4. Ramadan demands total abstinence from food, drink, smoking and sex between dawn and sunset over a full lunar month. It ends with the traditional festival of Eid al-Fitr.
5. Hajj, the holy pilgrimage to Mecca, is to be made at least once in every life. The rites begin and end at the Kabah, the square shrine believed to have been built by Abraham and his first son Ishmael. Final prayers take place at the Mount of Mercy, where the Prophet preached in the desert. This is followed by the three-day festival of Eid al-Adha

The Koran says 'Remembering God is what makes hearts find peace'. Islam means 'surrender to Allah', which simplifies their basic religion to most followers.

Muhammad's death in 632 left a vacuum in leadership never resolved. First, Abu Bakr, his father-in-law and close companion, was elected caliph in Medina. In 656 Muhammad's cousin and son-in-law Ali was accepted as leader by his Shi'a (partisans), supported in Iraq but resisted in Syria. Assassinated by a disillusioned follower, his son Hussein led a revolt, only to be killed at Karbala. Shi'ites regard him as a martyr. The Imams now followed, loyal followers of Ali. They are revered by the Shi'ites and maintain unity, peace and social justice.

But in 749 a new dynasty moved their capital from Damascus to Baghdad under a new ruler of the family of Muhammad's uncle Abbas. Unfortunately each of the 12 imams was murdered. The last is expected to return at the end of time as the Mahdi, to bring peace and unity.

Sunni Islam became the dominant tradition. They maintain that all should obey Allah's commands without question. They define a Muslim as anyone making the shahada, profession of faith: 'There is no god but God, and Muhammad is his messenger'. The ulamat (religious scholars) lead the Sunni with varying versions of right behaviour.

About 90 per cent of Muslims are Sunnis with varying cultures, including the hard-line Wahhabists in Saudi Arabia, and the Egyptian following of Sufi saints. Most concentrate strictly on commands of law. They regard the caliphs, successors of Muhammad, as authorities of the past history. They stress individual direct relations with Allah in public or private prayers. They accept marriage as inviolate.

Whereas Shi'ites are strong in the Yemen and Iran, elsewhere they are separated, tending to live in inaccessible mountainous regions. They honour Imanus, descended from Ali, Muhammad's son-in-law, and grandson Hussein, killed at Karbala in 680, as holy intercessors with Allah. Unlike Sunnis, they recognise temporary marriage and do not depend entirely on strictest interpretations of the law, developing their separate formulae.

12

THE FINAL QUESTION: DOES GOD REALLY EXIST?

Was there ever a God before the Creation, existing in a time- and spaceless void? Or a Supreme Spirit with cohorts of angels or lesser gods with specific tasks or duties? Possibly one such entrusted with the onus of creating our world, this Earth, to become a living entity. That leads to the conclusion that he shrouded his first creative efforts in such mystery that for the whole of mankind's existence, the search for clues to his early significance has proven fruitless. Nothing has ever been revealed or chronicled to enable us to discover how and when he shaped our world and its advancement. It remains impossible to prove or disprove his existence, despite all the manifest efforts of some of the greatest thinkers, philosophers and scientists. This most important boundless subject of a supernatural Being or Deity, creating and exercising power over nature and humans, has been discussed, debated, argued and even fought over through the centuries.

Scientists have been able to calculate the approximate age of our Earth and the probable emergence and stages of development of mankind. But the possibility of the primogenitor of a Deity and his responsibility remains only conjecture. The discoveries unearthed from digging into the distant past by archaeologists and geologists fill in many of the missing pieces of our heterogeneous jigsaw puzzle. Buried cities, graves, sepulchres, pyramids, have all revealed their ancient secrets to our wondering gaze. We are now able to picture and recompose whole dynasties, their people and their customs, and obtain a closer view of our primitive ancestors. Early theories have been confirmed of how *homo* first emerged and then developed in stages from *homo erectus* to *sapiens*. We now know their living habits, customs, clothing, weapons and tools, abilities and intelligence levels, even culture, from earliest pictograms to the first spoken language. Eventually the invention of first forms of writing, bringing the dawn of civilisation with records of daily life, accounts, bills, folklore, epics, all combine to enable us to trace our roots in our forebears.

Yet the greatest mystery of all remains completely unsolved: was there truly a God above and beyond the primitive man-made images of our ancestors? Has a real Supreme God existed always, unseen, intangible, impossible even to imagine or picture, who may have had some effect on our being, our lives and existence, without our knowledge? If so, why must we be denied sight, signal, sense, message or contact, to give us true comprehension and guidance? Just as we are expected to believe the existence of Moses' Ten Commandments, though no written record has ever been found – nor yet of the fantastic epic of Exodus and Moses' own great farewell. So we must apparently content ourselves with our precious gift of free will, without knowing whence it came, seemingly without inclusive forms of restraint or guidance. We have no proven concept of a God in any shape or form, or an overall Supreme Spirit. We are still left in complete ignorance, save for various vague suppositions.

There has never been evinced any real material or spiritual evidence to convince us at least of the possibility of such a Deity. We have all the fables, folklore, legends of our ancient ancestors with their polytheistic gods, personalised with carved images. The gods we inherited, transposed from those first

212

primitive idols, were supposedly supernatural beings, of whom Yahweh became accepted as the superior One God, above all others. Whether they believed in him or not, our ancestors still firmly retained and worshipped, and drew comfort from their earlier 'graven images'. Their continued existence was supposedly accepted by Yahweh, who claimed to be superior to and *above all other Gods...* yet threatened if they did 'bow down unto them or serve them' to 'visit the iniquity of the fathers upon the children, unto the third and fourth generation'. (Genesis 20:3–5) Should that terrible threat still hold, then woe betide those who still worship 'graven images' in their churches, cathedrals, temples, houses, meeting places, parks, even cemeteries. This must also include the man-made saints, still worshipped in human form. But that must diminish the credulity of all that follow but do not comprehend.

There is never mention of dissatisfaction by Yahweh with any of his animal, insect, fish or bird creation. Since their near-total destruction with the humans in that terrible, merciless drowning of almost the whole of his Creation, Yahweh seems to have turned his wrath completely upon the following generations of humans, descending from his champion Noah. They became no better than those destroyed because: 'It repenteth Me that I have made them'. (Genesis 6:7) Indeed they continued to annoy, irritate and displease him until he broke all his covenants and promises made to Noah, Abraham and the Patriarchs, Moses, the Elders and even directly to his 'Children of Israel', thereafter brutally destroying them just before their long-promised entry to his 'Promised Land'. He butchered all above 20 years old, together with their great leader, his loyal servant Moses (just for a whim of self-satisfaction because he was jealous), to be cast into some unknown grave. Was that the dignified conduct of a supreme Deity, purported worthy of total worship, trust and obedience? Or is such a God unacceptable, as later writers concluded?

Despite his obvious knowledge and experience of the frailty, weakness and fallibility of his human Creation, to whom he granted free will and then castigated them for exercising it, he continues to punish them harshly for their slightest offence. He sends plagues and disease, drowns Pharaoh's army (part of his Creation), utterly destroys Sodom and Gomorrah (instead of converting them), and is ever ready and willing to punish severely, kill, crush or murder, or cause bloody defeat and massacre, torture, annihilation, slavery, exile – there is no end to his stock of harsh punishments. After the golden calf worship at Sinai, he said to Moses: 'Now therefore let Me alone, that My wrath may wax hot against them, and that I may *consume* them.' (Exodus 32:10) Moses once again talks him round, so that he promises once more: 'Behold, I make a covenant; before all my people I will do marvels, such as have not been wrought in all the earth, nor in any nation.' (Exodus 34:10) Unfulfilled!

In fact, it was his demands upon *them* which grew out of all conception, given in the minutest details in Exodus, to be accomplished to perfection... with no thought about their weary situation in that desolate Wilderness. Not just his commandments and ordinances from Exodus 20, but in addition his detailed demands in 25–32, and 35–40, also the greater part of Leviticus and Deuteronomy, 248 commandments and 365 prohibitions. Impossible to absorb, commit to memory and carry out exactly, every minute demand of this tremendous burden imposed upon his suffering people. Yet when they grow tired of their daily dose of light manna and request more solid diet of meat and vegetables to uphold their strength, his anger knows no bounds. Like Alice's Queen he immediately cries: off with their heads: 'Take all the chiefs of the people and hang them up unto the Lord in face of the sun.' (Numbers 25:4)

Again in Numbers, he condemns them for expressing fear at the tales brought back by the spies, from the land of Canaan: 'I will smite them with the pestilence and destroy them' (Numbers 14:12) – and later: 'Your carcases shall fall in the wilderness, and all that were numbered of you – from twenty years old and upward – surely ye shall not come into the land. But as for you, your carcases shall fall in this wilderness.' (Numbers 14:29–32) He then orders a man caught gathering sticks on the Sabbath day to be: 'put to death; all the congregation shall stone him'. (Numbers 16:35) Again angered in Numbers 17:10: 'Get you up from among this congregation, that I may consume them in a moment'. He kills 24,000 by plague, who 'commit harlotry with the daughters of Moab'. (Numbers 25)

How could such a God be worthy of worship if he really existed? True the Prophets began reshaping him in a gentler, more merciful and even more sympathetically understanding mould, but still leaving in place all his myriad commandments and demands, with deadly threats against any disobedience. Even they could not remove the harsh side of his nature. The priests were prepared to accept him without question, as long as they gained the power they sought over the people. It took the learned rabbis of the 2nd century AD to remake his first harsh image with a more conciliatory, merciful, considerate but distant father figure Adonai, acceptable to future generations. But the Yahweh of the Beginning had still to be left in place in the set form of the earlier Old Testament, so to remain, with his exploits to be read with horror and disbelief by an increasing number of incredulous doubters, including the philosophers and men of reason, from the Middle Ages through the 17th to the 20th centuries.

From first to last we are expected by our religions to believe in, and worship and obey the behests of this unknown, unseen, unheard and invisible Spirit God, now supposedly all benevolence, goodwill and concern for any human distress or misfortune. Yet he still allows the most dreadful, destructive wars to erupt through world history, especially in the present era, causing untold misery, death, torture and destruction.

Many still prefer to remain neutral, waiting for proof to be vouchsafed one way or another. Since the first, original author who put pen to papyrus in the 10th century BC with his unique version of the Creation and its consequences, there have followed alterations and amendments to his text, especially concerning his anthropomorphic Yahweh. We must be specifically aware that the views of all three major religions, whilst acknowledging that they have a common source, differ as widely as all lay thinkers on this, the most interesting element of the Old Testament. Believers, non-believers, atheists, theists, polytheists, pantheists all have the same innate freedom to express their own views, and all differ.

The attempted changes from J's original anthropomorphic concept of Yahweh, and the amendments sought by his successors into the final century BC were deemed unacceptable, and the concept of God radically changed by the learned rabbis of the 2nd century AD. From J's original Yahweh to their infinite, unseen and unheard, merciful Adonai or Jehovah, finally inherited (apparently without criticism of such an enormous turnabout) from the dynamic, unyielding, heavily punishing, aggressive, intensely jealous Yahweh of Genesis and Exodus to Deuteronomy.

The foundation of the Pauline Church has also been subject to many changes in its progress to the Catholic hierarchy. Then to the major breakaway of the Protestant movement, which has been catastrophically decimated into so many different versions, some of short duration. Yet all supposedly worshipping the same God, whether One or Three, or Allah. All split not only from each other, but even more among themselves. So that one wonders whether they are now really concerned with the sole, monotheistic God of Abraham (Father of All Nations), or whether they are fighting for their own predominance over all other faiths and concepts of the Supreme Deity.

A.N. Wilson writes in *Paul: The Mind of the Apostle*: 'The fact that the Gentile world adopted Christianity is owing solely to one man, Paul of Tarsus. Without Paul it is highly unlikely that Christianity would ever have broken away from Judaism.' So Paul founded the 'Church militant'. But the 'Apostle to the Gentiles' is now rarely cited, and seems to have been dismissed by the Church of England for his many faults, e.g. that women should keep apart and silent in church and hide their hair; that slaves should obey their rulers because that is God's will.

Wilson says Paul 'seldom speaks of human beings loving God'. Paul's faith is that of 'urban people, far removed from the pastoral imagery of the Bible.' Paul believed the world was shortly coming to an end and could see no long-term existence for Christianity. In his world 'demonic powers were at work in a universe groaning and travailing towards some violent condemnation.' Wilson sees Paul as akin to such 19th-century spiritual exiles as Nietzsche and Kierkegaard, who have had much influence on 20th-century thought, seeing as absurd a picture of Christianity as an aid to social harmony. Yahweh's desire to keep Adam and Eve in a state of ignorance, bringing them terrible punishment and expulsion from Eden for disobedience, has been followed through all the years by the Church. Genesis foreshadows the eternal struggle between knowledge, science and religion.

The Catholic Church was especially strong against scientific knowledge, with persecution of those who dared to differ, and destruction of books of scientific knowledge or theory, and even the final threat of excommunication. Pope Urban VIII forced Galileo to recant his theory that the Earth moves round the Sun. Darwin's theories were dismissed as sacrilege by Wilberforce, Anglican Bishop of Oxford. The Church knew that scientists could not accept the literal truth of the Bible with its myths and folk tales. But Urban VIII and Wilberforce maintained that all faith was in vain if the Bible accounts of Creation were only allegories, expressing similar views to the early rabbis.

Many have now left the Church, dismayed by the deteriorating conditions – though some still retain their inherited unquestioned faith in a Supreme Being, vague, formless, but generally overseeing mankind's journey from birth till final demise. The only remaining hope, faint as yet, is for the leaders of all faiths to join together, before too late, to find an agreed solution and version acceptable to all the millions concerned. It may be too much to hope for a speedy agreement on a joint faith in one God or Supreme Spirit. An earnest desire, ecumenically expressed by leaders and congregations alike, could begin to move along the only valid path of full co-operation of all parties, to a final agreement to be accepted and augmented alike by all, in whatever form they finally agree. Who knows where this might lead? But what is certain is that unless a serious beginning be made soon, the churches, great temples, cathedrals, synagogues, mosques and other places of worship will finally become empty monuments for tourists and future historians to wonder at, and conjecture about our peculiar past history.

Voltaire's famous intriguing remark, 'If God did not exist, it would be necessary to invent him,' is just what has been done in a variety of guises, to suit differing concepts. Yet the

218

general and personal image remains vague and indefinable. How different from our ancestors in biblical times. They received a sharp whiplash to remind them to keep away from 'false gods', with dire punishments for any transgression. Much evil has been done since in the name of religion, through all the centuries into modern times – murder, assassination, even of priests, popes and rabbis, torture and wars killing millions – and modern extremists and fanatics still murdering, bombing and destroying just like their ancestors... plus ça change...

Nietzsche said: 'Since God is dead, everything is permitted.' This endeared him to Hitler and his evil Nazis, who misused him in their crude worship of pagan war gods, equally misrepresented from Wagner's overdrawn fantasies. But his nihilism remained unproven and, like Hitler, he also became mad.

Bertrand Russell said: 'Goodness is independent of God's decrees. If a moral code cannot be founded on authority, neither can it be founded on metaphysics, or on science or on imperial matters of fact. Why did God not endow men with a mature form of life, ensuring that they always behaved in ways that he approved? Because men have Free Will.' How can the sufferings that mankind endures be reconciled with the extreme benevolence now ascribed to God (compare the dreadful treatment meted out to poor, faithful Job, made to suffer in extremis for a wager between God and the devil)? Man's freedom of choice only vanishes with senility or slavery or incarceration. But the free exercise of man's will is often influenced by outside sources or pressures, family custom or habit. Our freedom may be diminished by emotional pressure under another's control (brainwashed or hypnotised), exposed to blackmail, torture or death. Some even follow their chosen 'media' as inspiration.

Practised or professional orators can convince men and women for good or evil, to sacrifice themselves for 'the good of the cause'. Religion can also exercise strong persuasion by semi-mystical ceremonies, even mass-control by television, persuading people to surrender their precious free will to the exhortations of newly arisen demi-gods. We may even behold godlike visions emerging from new computer machinery or the Internet.

Wars waged in the name and under the banner of one particular God, are not started by the people, engaged in their daily struggle for existence and family responsibilities. They are due to the ambitions of power-hungry, vain leaders, be they statesmen, dictators, heads of factions or religious authorities, convinced of their god-given rights. Strange that all ancient countries seem to have boasted their gods of war, to bolster man's primitive appetite for hunting and killing his prey. How quickly those primitive traits turn to hunting his fellow-men, with the pleasurable lust of battle inherited through the ages, brought to extremes of brutality, maiming and destruction in our present century.

One seeks in vain for gods of peace who would now command greater numbers of followers, sickened by the holocausts and cold-blooded mass murders of our time. Peace is such a fragile element, needing constant, devoted care and nourishment. Not by the gods who have permitted and watched over the murder of innocent men, women and babes, without taking any action to persuade or compel the slaughterers to cease their insane, bloody deeds. Such warlike gods cannot become gods of peace. Nor can leaders of wars become emissaries overnight of peaceful co-operation between all nations. What kind of religion is it that has its priests solemnly blessing the weapons of war on both sides in the name of the same God, and praying to the same God to give them victory over their fellow worshippers in the mass murders they have just countenanced? Should not our modern Pilates be forced to stay and face the truth of who and what is God, if he really does exist? It has produced a heartfelt desire for world peace from the survivors, but we are still subjected to the amoral direction of an ever-ready god of war.

Philosopher Hobbes rebels against Yahweh, asking: 'How can Christians believe the Creator gave Free Will to creatures made in his image, like a father... and then punish them for exercising that free will to his dissatisfaction?' Berman says: 'God is a Spirit and cannot become man, when he is by nature not related to his creatures at all. Therefore Christ's incarnation becomes physically impossible. There can be only ONE such Being, therefore the Holy Trinity is a misconception.' The 'Big Bang' cosmology (i.e. the science of the birth of the universe as a whole, in one quick action), questions: is God the sole creative cause of our origin? How can evil coexist with an omnipotent, wholly good Creator? (Yet primitive man believed in gods of good and evil.) In Plato's *Republic* the Supreme Good is matched by the Form and Power of the Real. Truth and Freedom then lead to perfection. Absolute standards of virtue exist, and goodness comes from true wisdom, but that does not constitute a god. Plato and Aristotle believed that morality, virtue and righteousness can be taught, and should be part of every curriculum. Aristotle said Plato was 'the man who showed how to be happy and good at the same time.' He extolled the virtues of righteousness and good thinking. But both agreed the necessity of a good social foundation.

Tillich emphatically repudiates the idea of a god who acts, who: 'brought the Universe into existence at a certain moment, governs it according to a plan, and directs it to an end.' Aristotle's God – ('Science is that which cannot be other

221

than it is – with the exception of stars and planets') – had nothing in common with the God of the Sermon on the Mount: 'There is much problematic about the kind of concept of God that helps to define the Mosaic traditions of Judaism, Christianity and Islam.' But theists and atheists both strongly believe in an orderly universe. Who then created it or ordered its composition? Man's freedom is fundamental to free will and progress. Freedom to think, study, decide to act when and where. Without it, there could be neither religion nor ethics. Matter itself has no life. The principle of existential causality is that every being has a reason or cause for its existence. Free will and freedom to think and act, supported by experience, still need a moral ethical base, but not necessarily a godhead. Aristotle demanded proof, insisting on the reality of logical thinking and the need to know by factual proof.

Electricity is the functioning power without which our world could not exist. Mankind could not function nor survive without it. Electricity provides the support that prevents a star collapsing on itself from its own gravity. The anthropic principle is that life will be possible only in those universes in which the right conditions exist. Non-existence cannot cause existence, but existence itself is unlimited. Whilst one may not accept the proffered concept of God the great Creator and progenitor, exerting spiritual influence from on high, there is no difficulty in conception of life as the natural flow of nature's forces with our ability to think, decide and act, written into our human code. There is no evidence of any guidance or prescription from any outside source.

Scientific accounts of our origins contradict most ethical values, shaped mainly by our religious heritage. This leaves the world and mankind in need of forms of justice and moral and ethical control. Without such moral precepts firmly incul-

222

cated, mankind would be doomed. We cannot accept the presupposition of Genesis that the quest for knowledge is wrong, nor the intolerant condemnation by Yahweh from Eden to a sorry state of lifelong struggle. Knowledge, pure or empiric, ever-sought, brings true understanding and contentment, especially when based on experience, which engenders wisdom and understanding.

The problem now arises that whereas scientists will argue amicably amongst themselves in all their branches and research, the Church is hopelessly split and in disagreement on the different approaches to faith and religious belief. The Church is slowly coming to terms with scientists and trying to bridge the ever-widening gap between science and faith, experience and belief, to find a rôle for ethics and morals and development of goodness rather than evil in mankind. But many still mask their indifference or unbelief by regular attendance at services and social occasions under the religious umbrella. Hypocrisy assumes many different disguises. 'To thine own self be true' is the wisest dictum, albeit the most difficult to follow.

Our universe is considered to be slowly moving towards finality. This may arrive suddenly should we receive a mighty blow from an outside body, as has happened before, wiping out dinosaurs and almost all creatures. If that be true, how can there be belief in a universal God who has not been able (or willing) to prevent previous catastrophes and loss of life or, like J's Yahweh, have wished upon mankind, like the floods, plagues and violent destruction of which he was so fond? Our primitive ancestors, in their ignorance of the elements and the causes of changes between day and night, and the reason for seasonal changes in the growth of plants, made gods of nature and, fearing the unknown, worshipped and sacrificed to them.

223

Similarly, belief in God is often the result of moral teaching and incentives, and fear of future punishment or hope of reward. We receive so much inherited way of thinking and behaviour that we too often accept such inherited moral standards and habits without question. But the quickening discoveries of scientists are now forcing us to review our previously accepted teaching and customs, and to think more deeply and personally of the meaning of life and its causes, and where it leads, to what future. Without any aid or guidance from an invisible, silent, supernatural being, to whom we turn in vain.

Philosophy, the love of wisdom, predominated with the ancient Greeks, who were influenced by the principles and thinking of the ancient Hebrews. Plato especially is claimed by Kabbala to incorporate much of their teaching in his philosophy, as also Pythagoras who, in addition to numerology and geometry, taught the transmigration of souls. On seeing a man beating a dog, he begged him to desist, as he was sure he recognised the voice of a friend in the dog's yelping. It first embraced all subjects, an enormously wide field as exemplified by Aristotle.

For the Greeks, philosophy meant the unity of eternal truths to provide the answers to all questions, including the possible existence of God, the nature of human knowledge and the good life for man. Naturalism is the implicit feature in all philosophies. It propounds the thinking of mankind in a natural world. Reason could lead mankind to perfection, given the evidence or experience to use the knowledge gained. Aristotle established a 'ladder of nature', progressing from inanimate matter, through plants and animals to man, the rational animal. Plato agreed with him that man, though rational, had irrational tendencies, whilst emerging from ordered nature.

224

Epistemology attempts, but fails to answer the question: what is knowledge and where does it come from? How do we acquire knowledge of right and wrong? How do we know God exists, and what is he like? A negative question, presupposing a negative answer. Metaphysics, called the 'science of being', seeks to establish a method of clarification of all human thought and knowledge, especially of God. Originated by Plato 'after the physics' because it came after his writings on physics, it discusses the limits of human thought and seeks to establish a spiritual being: 'All men by nature need to know. But we cannot move from the possibility of God to the reality of God without proof, and proof is not forthcoming.'

All very wise, but philosophy is not a kind of superior science, able to answer difficult questions like: is there a God? Do human beings survive their death? 'All philosophies are social criticism in their origin and consequences.' As I remember, much of student study of the subject consisted of destructive criticism of the work of the great philosophers, who were generally negative on the proposition 'Is there a God' or 'Did God ever exist, or was he a personficiation of nature?'

Frederick Copleston S.J. (*History of Philosophy*) says Jewish theology teaches that God is personal, but at the same time Pure Being, absolutely simple, free and self-sufficient. He does not occupy space or place but rather contains all things within Himself (Vol 1). Philo of Alexandria (died 40 AD) maintained that the same truth is to be found in both the Jewish Scriptures and tradition, and the Greek philosophy. He claimed that the Greek philosophers had made much use of the Sacred Scriptures.

Heraclitus' attitude to God was pantheistic. He said asses prefer straw to gold. All things are in a state of flux, constantly changing. Reality is One – but many at the same

225

time. He calls the 'One God and Wise God', the Universal Reason. But there is nowhere mentioned the Hebrew practice of allegorising the Scriptures and responding to questions with questions.

D.J. O'Connor agrees that philosophy is not a body of knowledge, but rather an activity of criticism or clarification showing what the problems are. It is not positive study like history, geology or law. It asks questions: is there a God, and if so what can we learn or infer about his nature? Do we survive death? Are we free to choose our own course of action? By what standards may we judge the right or wrong of human action, and who sets the standards? What is the difference between philosophical questions and those of logic or science? What sort of evidence do we employ to advance our knowledge? How do we measure time, which remains one of the world's greatest mysteries, an eternal puzzle like the so-called laws of nature and energy? Stephen Hawking says that time becomes another dimension of space — but he does not offer any true method of calculating time. We are left without knowledge of what time really is, and can only measure by physical change, like the moving mechanism of a clock, but not its real essence.

Philosophy does not propound the proof that Aristotle demanded. Reason was esteemed by the Greeks as the noblest of all faculties. Belief seeks to solve the eternal mystery and paradox of the human condition, rising above reason, logic and the factual. In the ultimate, mankind needs the intangible, inexpressible belief in something beyond human conjecture. This is our inheritance from our earliest ancient, inarticulate ancestors who worshipped the first mysterious spirit forms of life and fertility.

Dr Christopher Corbally, British Vice-Director of the Vatican observatory in Arizona, is quoted as saying in 1997 that our image of God will have to change if evidence of alien life on Mars is confirmed by scientists. 'The modern concept of an anthropocentric God may have to evolve into a broader entity, to take account of the insights of any intelligent alien culture. We need a proper sense of God, one derived in the dialogue between religion and science. It would give us a sense of being an integral part of a cosmic community. We would discover a church far beyond the confines of the Earth and of any narrow interpretation of the Bible or other scriptures.' Evidence that the Catholic Church is moving out of its erstwhile narrow confines, convinced by all the continuous scientific discoveries, not only on the origin of mankind, but also on the possible relationship between science and hitherto accepted beliefs.

What then is normal behaviour? The basis of education is not only to teach, but also to guide people to think for themselves and seek the right way forward, and to draw out their better instincts for good. It is hoped thereby to develop a better and more ethical code of behaviour. Then with ability properly established, to judge between right and wrong, people should be left free to choose their course of conduct. The existence of a deity exacting retribution for the slightest fault, or promising reward in a future life or existence, has not been established, despite the efforts of the severe, anthropomorphic figure of the original Yahweh of the Pentateuch. Hume held no belief in the possibility of a future life, but accepted the conjecture that a person might assume different identities in future existence, as advanced by Pythagoras, Buddhism and the Kabbala. But again, this is all conjecture. If there be a God or Supreme Spirit, unknown, invisible, with no direct relationship with mankind, then there exists no means of communication except through the semi-mystical profession of faith, as preached by the Church, itself split into many differing factions with

227

conflicting doctrines. Hardly a fit and proper guide to a Supreme Spirit!

We now refute any validity of ancient mythical legends of Creation, and the imaginative authorship that produced from them such implausible stories as the birth and procreation of Adam and Eve and their first family and descendants. Then the mythological accounts of the Flood and Babel, culled from previous epic tales from Sumerian, Babylonian and other sources. Even the implausibility of Isaac's birth at Abraham's age of 100 and Sarah barren at 90, followed by Abraham's willingness to sacrifice his only son's life at the behest of Yahweh. The struggle (matching previous tales) of Isaac's twins, followed by the mysterious night-long struggle for his life by Jacob against Yahweh's emissary. The violent destruction of Sodom and Gomorrah (maybe an earthquake), preceded by the impossible bargaining scene amicably conducted between Yahweh and Abraham as they walked together down the road to Sodom. The incredible dream stories of Joseph followed by the reality of the harsh brutality of Pharaoh, then the miracles and plagues to convince Pharaoh. However, there is a sense of reality in the escape of those long-suffering Hebrew slaves from their long penury – followed by their hard battles across the great stretch of land called Canaan to reach the 'Promised Land', which was running with blood rather than milk and honey.

Their hard-won victories even after reaching Palestine – the tremendous feats of their greatest King and leader David (without the fairytale of the shepherd-boy's slingshot victory over giant Goliath). The rise and fall of Israel, with their enemies' renewal after defeats, only to be finally destroyed by the wilful acts of their acknowledged One God Yahweh, because they dared to stray from his sole worship, seems almost fact becoming myth. So much has to be seen as ancient legend, mythology and folklore (like the fanciful exaggerated media accounts which appear with our modern wars and events), added to the educated intelligent imagination of that outstanding original author J from Jerusalem, who was responsible for production of the Epic of birth and development of Judaism from its mythical inception.

A.C. Bouquet, in *Comparative Religion*, maintains that the Deity uses the Hebrews as: 'His instrument for making known His nature and purpose. The Hebrew God is omnipotent and transcends the entire universe. He needs no images, no temples, nor ornate altars. He is of infinite holiness and majesty, and the perfection of moral goodness. Hence he has no pleasure in ritual sacrifices and no need of them. A life of habitually right conduct... observance of the divinely appointed moral law and the practice of a neighbourly spirit of good will towards one's fellow-men, are the only sacrifice God needs.' Bouquet's philosophy is shared by many who seek a simple faith, uncluttered by ornate images and ceremonies. But his Deity is far removed from the Yahweh of the Pentateuch.

Still the problem remains unsolved by prophets and priests as to why such a theoretical God allows so much pain and suffering for mankind to endure. D.H. Lawrence said: 'Jesus trusted in God and God let him down.' It must be admitted that all religions began with a mythical foundation, with a mystical quality in their 'Beginning' birth-pangs, until strong development formulated actuality. At least these three great religions of Judaism, Christianity and Islam have stood the test of time. They should now co-operate to return to the original foundation of Abraham, if they are to survive – on a newly constituted basic faith of reason and righteousness and equality.

It must be left to each individual to find the way forward to suit his or her own philosophy, after due consideration of all the options and possibilities resulting from personal thoughts, meditation and experience. It is all vast conjecture with no perfect solution. Better then to hold to the simple basic tenets of guidance through life. Hear no evil, think no evil, seek no evil, but seek only good and righteousness, and try to follow the Ten Commandments as the foundation stone of human existence. Above all to follow one's own conscience.

ACKNOWLEDGEMENTS

I owe special thanks to a host of fine authors whose erudite works I have studied, analysed, plundered or argued with, whilst trying to formulate my thoughts into some form of cohesion. Professors H. Bloom and David Rosenberg, whose *Book of J* helped to guide me along their well laid-out paths, introducing me to this fabulous first author, to whom we owe the foundation of our Bible, and of special mention:

Henrietta McCall:	*Mesopotamian Myths*
Abba Eban:	*Heritage, with deep admiration for a 'whole' man*
T.H. Gaster:	*Myths*
A.J. Ayer:	*The Claims of Theology*
Richard Leakey:	*The Origins of Humankind*
John D. Barrow:	*The Origin of the Universe*
J. Miete and A. Flew:	*Does God Exist* – a well-conducted deep debate, like true philosophers ending in a draw
George Hart:	*Egyptian Myths*
Henry O. Thompson:	*Bible Archaeology*
Stephen Hawking:	*A Brief History of Time*
A.N. Wilson:	*Paul: The Mind of the Apostle*
The British Encyclopaedia	
British Museum:	*Sumerians*
Bertrand Russell:	*History of Western Philosophy*
A.C. Bouquet:	*Comparative Religion*

231

Hans-Joachim Schoops:	*Intelligent Man's Guide to the Religions*
Frederick Copleston S.J. (my good friend and adviser):	*A History of Philosophy Vol 1*
Irwin Erdman:	*Four Ways of Philosophy*
The Bible	Fount of all knowledge, the ultimate 'Book of Books', encapsulating every aspect of mankind's journey through life.